House & Garden

Born in London in 1939, Alan Ayckbourn spent most of his childhood in Sussex and was educated at Haileybury. Leaving there one Friday at the age of seventeen, he went into the theatre the following Monday and has been working in it ever since as, variously, a stage manager, sound technician, scene painter, prop-maker, actor, writer and director. These talents developed thanks to his mentor, Stephen Joseph, whom he first met in 1958 upon joining the newly formed Library Theatre in Scarborough. He was a BBC Radio Drama producer from 1965 to 1970, returning to Scarborough to take up the post of Artistic Director of the Theatre in the Round, left vacant after Stephen Joseph's death in 1967. He has premièred over fifty of his plays at this Yorkshire theatre where he spends the greater part of the year directing other people's work. Some thirty of his plays have subsequently been produced either in the West End, at the Royal National Theatre or the Royal Shakespeare Company. They have been translated into forty different languages and have been performed throughout the world, receiving many national and international awards. Alan Ayckbourn was appointed a CBE in 1987 and in 1997 received a knighthood for services to the theatre.

WOMAN IN MIND (DECEMBER BEE)
MR A'S AMAZING MAZE PLAYS
INVISIBLE FRIENDS
THE REVENGER'S COMEDIES
TIME OF MY LIFE
WILDEST DREAMS
COMMUNICATING DOORS
THINGS WE DO FOR LOVE
COMIC POTENTIAL
THE BOY WHO FELL INTO A BOOK
ALAN AYCKBOURN: PLAYS ONE
(A Chorus of Disapproval, A Small Family Business,
Henceforward . . . , Man of the Moment)
ALAN AYCKBOURN: PLAYS TWO
(Ernie's Incredible Illucinations, Invisible Friends,
This Is Where We Came In, My Very Own Story,
The Champion of Paribanou)

adaptations
THE FOREST by Alexander Ostrovsky

ALAN AYCKBOURN

House & Garden

faber and faber

First published in 2000
by Faber and Faber Limited
3 Queen Square, London WC1N 3AU
Published in the United States by Faber and Faber Inc.
an affiliate of Farrar, Straus and Giroux Inc., New York

Typeset by Country Setting, Kingsdown, Kent CT14 8ES
Printed in England by Mackays of Chatham plc, Chatham, Kent

A CIP record for this book
is available from the British Library

ISBN 0–571–20593–3

2 4 6 8 10 9 7 5 3 1

Author's Note

House and *Garden* are two plays
intended to be performed simultaneously
by the same cast in two adjacent auditoria.
They can be seen singly and in no particular order.

Revisions made to the text during rehearsals for
the production at the Royal National Theatre
are not included in this edition.

House & Garden was first performed at the Stephen
Joseph Theatre, Scarborough, on 17 June 1999.
The cast was as follows:

Teddy Platt Robert Blythe
Trish Platt Eileen Battye
Sally Platt Charlie Hayes
Giles Mace Barry McCarthy
Joanna Mace Janie Dee
Jake Mace Danny Nutt
Gavin Ryng-Mayne Terence Booth
Barry Love Simon Green
Lindy Love Alison Senior
Lucille Cadeau Sabine Azema
Fran Briggs Alexandra Mathie
Warn Coucher Peter Laird
Izzie Truce Antonia Pemberton
Pearl Truce Jennifer Luckraft

Maypole Dancers and Bandsmen

Director Alan Ayckbourn
Designer Roger Glossop
Lighting Designer Mick Hughes
Costume Designer Christine Wall
Music John Pattison

A new production was subsequently presented at the
Royal National Theatre, London, on 9 August 2000.
The cast was as follows:

Teddy Platt David Haig
Trish Platt Jane Asher
Sally Platt Charlie Hayes
Giles Mace Michael Siberry
Joanna Mace Sian Thomas
Jake Mace James Bradshaw
Gavin Ryng-Mayne Malcolm Sinclair
Barry Love Adrian McLoughlin
Lindy Love Suzy Aitchison
Lucille Cadeau Zabou Breitman
Fran Briggs Alexandra Mathie
Warn Coucher Peter Laird
Izzie Truce Antonia Pemberton
Pearl Truce Nina Sosanya

Maypole Dancers and Bandsmen

Director Alan Ayckbourn
Set Designer Roger Glossop
Lighting Designer Mick Hughes
Costume Designer Christine Wall
Music John Pattison

HOUSE

Characters

Teddy Platt, a businessman
Trish Platt, his wife
Sally Platt, their daughter
Giles Mace, a doctor
Joanna Mace, his wife, a teacher
Jake Mace, their son, a student reporter
Gavin Ryng-Mayne, a novelist
Barry Love, a shopkeeper
Lindy, his wife, a shopkeeper
Lucille Cadeau, an actress
Fran Briggs, her driver
Warn Coucher, a gardener
Izzie Truce, a housekeeper
Pearl Truce, an occasional cleaner
Several children of about seven or eight years old

Scene: the summer sitting room at the house.

Time: a Saturday in August between eight o'clock in the morning and six in the evening.

Act One

Saturday, August 14th, 8.00 a.m.

The summer sitting room at the house.

It is an impressive ground-floor room at the back of a Georgian building which overlooks the terrace and small formal garden. Beyond this is a flight of stone steps leading down to the less formal Lower Meadow beyond.

The room itself has a number of floor to ceiling windows, two of them French windows which lead onto the terrace. It is comfortably furnished in the tastefully shabby, cluttered, casual English country house tradition.

Two other doors lead off, one to the hall and rest of the house; and double doors into the dining room. These latter are normally closed but, when open, the end of what appears to be a long dining table can be seen.

In a moment, Trish, a woman in her forties whose soft English beauty has only very faintly faded, enters from the hall. She surveys the room and its clutter, sighs, sniffs the air with mild distaste, goes to the French windows and opens them.

She makes for the hall door again, then pauses to pick something up, straighten a cushion. A token gesture towards tidying the untidyable.

As she does this Teddy, a rather red-faced man also in his forties, appears outside the French windows. He is wearing old clothes and boots.

Teddy I'm just taking Spoof for a run in the meadow. Alright?

Trish continues her tidying, appearing neither to hear nor see Teddy at all.

So, if anyone phones, can you take a message? Tell 'em I'll ring 'em back in a minute. OK?

No response.

Trish?

Trish finishes what she is doing and goes into the dining room.

(*as she goes*) It's just possible Ryng-Mayne may call to give me an update when he'll – (*as it becomes apparent that she is not hearing him*) Oh, for God's sake, Trish! We can't keep on like this, woman! Trish!

She has gone.

(*yelling after her*) This is a very important day for me, you know. If you cock it up for me, I'll never forgive you. Do you hear me, Trish?

Outside somewhere Spoof, a large dog, barks with pleasure at the sound of his master's voice.

Alright, Spoof, that'll do! Spoof! Stop that at once!

Spoof barks happily on.

Spoof! (*giving up, muttering*) Oh, give me strength! I don't know. I'm the bloody invisible man round here. Nobody takes a blind bit of notice. Might as well not be here at all. Just a hole in the ether these days.

He starts to go. So does Spoof.

(*as he goes*) SPOOF! Will you just simmer down, you stupid dog.

They have gone. Silence in the empty room for a second. Then Sally enters from the hall. She is Trish and Teddy's only child. Seventeen and still at school, she is a serious, sometimes rather intense girl who has recently grown very concerned with Life and

The World. She is wearing her school uniform and carries a briefcase. She comes into the room and stops, listening. She frowns.

She sits on the sofa and opens her briefcase. She pulls out a sheet of paper and studies it.

Sally (*reading, softly and dramatically*)
How can I ever hear a heart,
My head denies with such insistence?
How do I ever trust a heart,
Which doubt drowns out with such persistence?
How will I ever feel my heart,
Whilst caution proffers such resistance?
How could I ever give my heart
When I deny its whole existence?

Trish returns. Sally hastily returns her poem to the briefcase.

Trish Oh, good morning, Sally . . . Were you talking to me?

Sally No. What was all that about just now?

Trish When?

Sally Was that Dad . . .?

Trish . . . What are you doing, up and dressed?

Sally . . . I heard him shouting . . .

Trish . . . It's not even midday.

Sally . . . Yelling his head off.

Trish . . . What are you up to? It's Saturday, had you forgotten?

Sally I've got a meeting at nine. Don't say you didn't hear him?

Trish No. I heard Spoof.

Sally Yes. And Dad.

Trish No, I only heard Spoof.

Sally gives up with a sigh.

I think we'll have to use the big table. We always have this problem, don't we? The small table's too small and the large table's too large. We either have to have three people to lunch or forty-six. What meeting's this, then?

Sally Up at the school.

Trish Oh, is that why you're all dressed up?

Sally I'm dressed up because we have enlightened teachers who encourage all sorts of activities outside normal school hours but a reactionary head teacher who won't allow any pupil on the premises unless they're in school uniform . . .

Trish What's the meeting? Anything important?

Sally Senior Political Group.

Trish Oh. We'll never get seven of us round the small table. We'd all be eating off each other's plates. (*Trish starts to move around in the dining room as she tries out various table lay-outs using table mats as markers. Occasionally she vanishes from sight, sometimes stopping in the doorway to speak to Sally directly.*)

Sally Have I got to be here? For lunch?

Trish You certainly have.

Sally I could eat in the kitchen . . .

Trish You'll eat with us . . .

Sally . . . if it would help. I could eat with Izzie.

Trish Sally, you're eating with us, please.

8

Sally Thought it might help, that's all.

Trish Well, it wouldn't . . . I need you to . . . converse and . . . pass things . . . (*lingering in the dining room doorway, surveying the table*) No, I'll put us all up this end. If we're spread out, we'll be yelling our heads off.

Sally French film stars are not exactly my strong point, you know . . .

Trish Nor mine. That's beside the point. You speak French, anyway . . .

Sally . . . I mean, I haven't even seen her film . . :

Trish I don't think anyone's seen her film. Not round these parts . . .

Sally . . . Jake probably has . . .

Trish . . . By the time they get round to showing a film here most of the stars are dead . . .

Sally . . . Jake's bound to have seen it. What's it called, anyway?

Trish The – hang on, I did know – *The Un* – *The Un* – something or other.

Sally Is it French?

Trish No, English, I think. Well, American.

Sally And how come she's in this neck of the woods?

Trish I'm not quite sure. She was suggested by her agent. Our committee originally wanted the other one – that very famous one who was also in the film. But she was unexpectedly unavailable – *The Unexpected*, that's it! – so they suggested this one instead. Lucille – thingy. Who isn't really famous at all but is apparently very, very good. According to her agent.

9

Sally Just nobody's ever heard of her.

Trish Don't ask me, I've never heard of anybody. Anyway, she's agreed to open our fête which was more than the other one was, which makes her OK in my book. Can you man the tombola as usual, please?

Sally Oh, you're not going to make me stand out there all afternoon in the pouring rain like last year, are you?

Trish It's not going to rain . . .

Sally Of course it's going to rain . . .

Trish Nonsense. The forecast says –

Sally . . . It always rains. Last year that tombola drum was full of water. All the tickets were floating . . .

Trish Come on, Sally, for goodness sake. Lighten up, darling. Everything's such an effort, isn't it? You're young. Enjoy that while it lasts.

Sally Standing in the rain?

Trish That's all part of it . . .

Sally Selling soggy tickets for prizes people won last year and have put back this year, praying they won't win them again?

Trish Absolutely. All part of the fun.

Sally (*softly mocking*) When I was your age . . .

Trish Yes, alright.

Sally (*continuing*) We used to dance all day. On the lawn. In our nightdresses. (*after a pause*) I'm amazed you still bother, really.

Trish How do you mean?

Sally With all – this . . . going on?

Trish What?

Sally All this – that we're not supposed to talk about but we all know about anyway.

Trish I don't know what you mean.

Sally I've noticed.

Trish What time's this meeting of yours?

Sally You two want to get yourselves sorted out, you know. Instead of giving me lectures on lightening up.

Trish If it's at nine o'clock you'd better get moving . . .

Sally You hear what I'm saying, Mum? I'm serious.

Trish . . . You know what the buses are like on Saturdays.

Sally Jake's collecting me. Listen, if you –

Trish You take advantage of him far too much, as well.

Sally What?

Trish Jake. He trails round after you like a lost puppy. You just use him when it suits you.

Sally (*indignantly*) I do not.

Trish Yes, you do.

Sally I don't ask him to follow me around, do I?

Trish You don't send him away either, do you?

Sally It's what makes him happy.

Trish It's called using people, Sally. They – care about you, you care nothing for them but you use them because it suits you.

Sally That's terrible. What a terrible thing to say!

Trish It's alright. I'm not blaming you especially. Lots of us have done it. All I'm saying is, try not to. For one reason, it'll rebound on you later. It always does.

Sally What are you talking about?

Trish I'm saying that – in my experience – life pays you back. Sooner or later. Believe me, I know. You behave badly . . . thoughtlessly towards someone . . . as if their feelings weren't important . . . then one day . . .

Sally They behave like that to you? Well, I'm not letting that happen to me, I can tell you that. Never lose control. That's the secret, keep control.

Trish Of other people?

Sally No, of myself. Don't let yourself get used, get manipulated, taken advantage of. And of course, no, don't do it to others either. Which I don't, as it happens. I don't use them, not at all.

Trish Even more alarming if you don't even realise you're doing it. (*back at her table*) Yes, we'll lay it up like that.

Sally It's another get Sally morning, isn't it? And don't you dare put me next to that man, either.

Trish What's that?

Sally Gavin whosit-whatsit. I'm not sitting next to him.

Trish Why on earth not? I seem to remember he was very charming.

Sally Oh, yes?

Trish Novelist, political wheeler dealer. Right up your street, I'd have thought.

Sally Sorry. Hardly my kind of politics, mother.

Trish Oh, well. Karl Marx wasn't free for lunch, unfortunately.

Sally Really . . . I'd love to know what he's doing here.

Trish He's coming for lunch.

Sally What, travelling two hundred miles from London just to have lunch? All this I'm-an-old-friend-of-Dad's. Highly suspicious.

Trish (*dryly*) Being a contradiction in terms, you mean?

Sally Listen. Seriously, if you want to talk about things, about what's happening . . . It affects all of us. Not just you, Dad and Joanna. But there's Jake's father as well, isn't there? There's Giles. And then there's Jake. (*Slight pause.*) I am thinking about other people, you see. (*Pause.*) And me. There's me. You see? So we have to talk, don't we?

Trish I don't know whether to use the cloth or the plain wood with mats. This surface is totally wrecked. We should never have used it as a ping pong table . . .

> *At this moment Jake, about nineteen or twenty years old, appears on the terrace. He is shy, slightly nervous and clearly besotted with Sally.*
> *Sally sees him. Jake waves through the window to indicate that he's there.*

Sally (*seeing Jake*) Oh, hallo . . .

Jake (*tentatively entering the room*) Hi!

Trish Who's that? Oh, Jake. Good morning.

Jake Good morning.

Trish I'll shut the door. Leave you in peace. Sally's got something to say to you.

Jake Has she?

Trish closes the dining room doors. Sally has opened her briefcase and is sorting through some papers.

I parked the car down by the gate. Walked up through the garden.

Sally Why d'you do that?

Jake Well, I just thought . . . it might be nice . . . for us to . . . walk through the garden. (*looking out*) Seeing as it's such a . . . it's a . . . as it's not raining.

Pause.

What did you want to tell me, then?

Sally What?

Jake Your mother said you had something to say to me.

Sally Did she?

Jake What is it, then?

Sally I've no idea. Ask her. (*She studies her papers.*)

Jake What's that?

Sally It's my speech.

Jake Ah.

Sally For the meeting. I was up half the night with it. Some of them are so stupid, if you don't spell things out in words of one syllable . . .

Jake (*sympathetically*) Yes. I know, our features editor always says –

Sally What I'm trying to get across, is that in politics, any sort of politics, local or national – these days it's tactics. It isn't always simply a question of voting for what you want . . .

Jake No.

Sally Sometimes you have to vote for what you positively don't want in order to achieve the longer term aim of getting something you do want. You see?

Jake Tactical voting?

Sally (*waving a sheet of paper*) Fact. Colin Theaker is the most unpopular MP this constituency has had since records were started. He wasn't that popular when he was elected and in four and a half years he's managed to halve that support. Pretty remarkable even for Colin Theaker . . .

Jake I know. We ran that article recently . . .

Sally Mind you, he's a crook, which doesn't help.

Jake Well, we don't know that for certain . . .

Sally He is. He's a crooked little shit.

Jake You're not going to say that in your speech, are you?

Sally Of course I'm not. But even his own party which is made up almost entirely of crooks is a little nervous about him. They'd replace him tomorrow only if they did it would amount to a tacit admission they knew he was a crook. The point is if Theaker remains their candidate at the General Election there could be a complete turn-round. They could find themselves out on their ear. The whole lot of them. We'd be in. For the first time. Ever. Think of that.

Jake Lot of ifs.

Sally Dave Bales could be our next MP. Think of that.

Jake Yes, I met him once. He's OK, he's quite –

Sally But you see if that's to happen, it's vital they're not panicked into replacing Theaker. With someone with a bit more – someone new who might just swing it for them.

Jake They might replace him anyway.

Sally They might. I think it's unlikely. That would be a virtual admission that some of the rumours about him are true. No, they'll stick with him if they possibly can. So. QED. I'm going to propose we cool our campaign. Which isn't going to be very popular with some of our lot. But you see my point?

Jake Theaker must stay?

Sally For the time being. Still. Sixth Form Senior Political Society. What are we going to change?

Jake Voters of the future.

Sally Sure. We've been given a voice, use it.

Jake I feel a bit sorry for Theaker, actually.

Sally What? Come on . . .

Jake Well, he had a tough act to follow. Two tough acts. Your grandfather, your great-grandfather . . .

Sally Things were different in those days . . .

Jake Still, you can't help wondering. If, say, your father had decided to stand, for instance . . .

Sally Well, they asked him originally. Dad's not interested, though. Never has been. He told me once he thinks all politics are boring.

Jake You take after your grandfather . . .

Sally He had a passion, yes. I share the passion, if not the same views.

Jake Would you ever want to stand? As an MP?

Sally Maybe. One day. Who knows? If I thought I could be useful. I'd be a very good one. Change things for the better.

Jake (*adoringly*) You'd be fantastic.

Sally Come on, I'm going to be late. (*She starts to pack up her things.*)

Jake I saw them again just now, by the way. My mother and your father.

Sally Oh, God. Where?

Jake In the garden. As usual.

Sally Where did you see them . . .? They weren't – you know – ?

Jake Oh, no. They were just standing about. Pretending to talk about bushes, you know.

Sally I don't know what we do, Jake. I really don't. I've tried talking to my mother but she won't even acknowledge it's happening.

Jake How about your father?

Sally I gave up talking to him years ago. After what he's done to my mother, I never want to speak to him again. Have you managed to talk to your mother, yet?

Jake No, she's . . . She's – quite an emotional sort of person, you know . . .

Sally Yes, I have noticed. If you don't mind my saying so, I think she's seriously unstable, actually . . .

Jake Well. Maybe a bit. And my father – I'm sure he still doesn't know.

Sally That's incredible. Where does he live? In a plastic bag?

Jake No, he's . . . well, he trusts her, you see. He trusts most people. Actually, he trusts everyone, that's the trouble. The thing about my father is – well, it sounds a bit boring but I think he's just a very, very nice man.

Sally He's a bloody sight nicer man than my father, anyway. Oh, what's the point of talking about it? They'll have to sort it out between them. There's nothing we can do.

Jake I wish there was, though. I was wondering if . . . Are you going to be at the fête this afternoon . . .?

Sally Unfortunately. Or risk the wrath of my mother . . .

Jake I was just wondering – because I'm going to have to be there – I've got to interview this film actress, you see – and I just wondered, you know – if afterwards – if you – if you – we could drive out to this place I –

Sally Probably not this evening, Jake.

Jake Right.

Sally I have – lots to do. Revision and so on.

Jake Yes.

Sally Shall we go?

Jake Sure, I cleaned the car out, by the way. You'll be relieved to hear. I know last time you said it smelt a bit odd . . .

Sally It did. Disgusting.

Jake I think it was some old pizza. I found it under the passenger seat . . .

They are just going out of the French windows when they meet Teddy coming back in.

Teddy (*to Sally*) Oh, hallo. What are you doing up this early? Been a fire drill, has there?

Sally walks past him, totally ignoring him.

Jake She's just going to a meeting.

Teddy Is she? What's that? WI's?

Jake Political, I think.

Teddy (*yelling after her*) Waste of time! Complete waste of time!

Jake (*as he goes*) I'm driving her there.

Teddy Jolly good.

Sally and Jake are gone. Teddy is alone in the room for a second. The dining room doors open abruptly and Trish sticks her head out.

Trish Would you both like a cup of – (*She looks round the room and appears to see no one.*) – Oh, nobody here.

Trish closes the doors again before Teddy can speak.

Teddy (*angrily*) Oh, for God's sake! (*He marches to the dining room doors and flings them open. Trish is not in view. Shouting into the apparently empty room*) I'm not putting up with this much longer, you know. I've had just about enough!

Their housekeeper, Izzie, comes in from the hall. She is a woman, probably in her late fifties, stern-faced and unsmiling. Somebody who feels their lot to be less than a happy one.

Izzie You calling me, were you?

Teddy No, no, Izzie. I was just – talking to my wife. In the dining room.

Izzie (*looking into the dining room*) She's not in here.

Teddy Isn't she? Well, fancy that.

Izzie I'll shut these doors.

Teddy Fine.

Izzie So Pearl can get on hoovering in there.

Teddy Right.

Izzie (*closing the dining room doors*) If she ever turns up.

Teddy Oh, dear. Gone AWOL again, has she?

Izzie Don't know where she's gone. Needs her feet nailing to the ground, that one. That or a father.

Teddy Bit late to find one of those for her, isn't it?

Izzie (*darkly, as she goes*) I'm working on it.

Teddy Listen, Izzie, I'm expecting Giles – Dr Mace to join me in a minute.

Izzie Oh, yes?

Teddy Could you make us some coffee when he comes?

Izzie Give me a call.

> *Izzie goes out. Teddy goes to the hall door. Opens it swiftly, listens, then closes it. He moves to the dining room doors and is about to do the same with them when they burst open and Trish comes out, now with gardening gloves and secateurs.*
>
> *Simultaneously, Giles appears on the terrace. He is a pleasant, affable, if somewhat ineffectual man in his late thirties.*

Teddy (*to Trish*) Oh, there you are. Will you kindly not walk away from me every time I –

> *But Teddy is seemingly invisible to Trish. She sweeps past him with no acknowledgement and straight out through the French windows.*

Trish Good morning, Giles. Bit early for lunch, aren't you?

Giles Good morning, Trish. No, I was looking for Teddy, actually. Is he – ?

Trish No idea, Giles. I haven't seen hide nor hair of him this morning, I'm afraid . . .

Giles Oh.

> *Trish has gone off towards the garden. Giles looks cautiously into the room and sees Teddy.*

(*a trifle surprised*) Ah!

Teddy (*grimly*) Did you witness that?

Giles What?

Teddy You see what I mean?

Giles Say again?

Teddy Clear evidence. With your own eyes. She comes in. I see her. I speak to her. She fails to reply, utterly ignores me. She goes out. Meets you. Greets you. You ask where I am. She says she hasn't seen me when less than five seconds earlier, she'd just walked straight past me. Tell me. Is that normal behaviour? Is that the decorum of a sane woman?

Giles See what you mean. Yes.

Teddy What's your opinion?

Giles Well, I'd have to examine her, of course. At least talk to her, but even then . . . It seems to me more of a . . . In the mind. As it were.

Teddy A basket case?

Giles No, no, no . . . I don't think that. I don't really know, really. Not having . . . talked to her, Teddy. But . . .

Teddy I appreciate as a professional you want to hedge your bets but at least you'll agree it's not usual?

Giles No. Not altogether usual . . .

Teddy For a wife to declare her husband invisible? That is abnormal behaviour. Surely? In anyone's book?

Giles It does happen but –

Teddy Does it?

Giles Occasionally.

Teddy Can you ever recall it happening?

Giles No, not off-hand . . .

Teddy Has it ever happened to you? With Joanna?

Giles Well, over brief periods. I mean that's marriage, isn't it? Over the years there are always sticky patches where you tend to ignore each other for a short while. Jo's gone a bit quiet on me now and then for a couple of hours sometimes but . . . How long's it been like this for you?

Teddy Three weeks.

Giles Yes, that is a long time, isn't it?

Teddy I mean, there's got to be something radically wrong, Giles, hasn't there? I mean, three weeks. I'm not a medical man, I don't know all the technical terms, but it doesn't take a brain surgeon to see she's out of her tree. She's bloody good at it, mind you. Very hard to catch her out. I made her blink once or twice but that doesn't mean anything. Apart from stamping on her foot I can't think of any way to catch her attention.

Giles What about – in bed?

Teddy Bed?

Giles Does she ignore you then?

Teddy I've no idea. We sleep in separate rooms.

Giles Ah. Sorry.

Teddy It was her idea. She claimed I was – disruptive in the night.

Giles I see. Teddy, I hate to suggest this, but do you think that that might be at the bottom of it?

Teddy Bottom of what?

Giles Well, bluntly, sex?

Teddy Well. Anything's possible where sex is concerned, I suppose.

Giles Frankly, and I don't want to sound too fiercely Freudian about all this, but I think I'd look to the sex, first and foremost.

Teddy You would?

Giles I would.

Teddy You think I ought to try and – get back into bed with her. Re-establish the territorial claim?

Giles I think you ought to – re-open negotiations, perhaps.

Teddy Right. She's in the garden at the moment, I don't think I should . . .

Giles Heavens, I wasn't talking about now.

Teddy Weren't you?

Giles I was thinking – tonight, perhaps.

Teddy Tonight? I can't wait till then.

Giles You can't?

Teddy No, listen, Giles. I'll have to tell you. This is absolutely hush-hush. Not a word to anyone.

Giles Right.

Teddy The point is, I've got someone rather important coming to lunch today . . .

Giles Oh yes, I know. Lucille Cadeau, the French film star. She's frightfully good. I saw her film when I was in London. *The Uninvited – Unprotected* – something like that. It's really excellent. Unfortunately she gets blown up quite early on . . .

Teddy No, Giles, Giles, I'm not talking about that woman. I'm talking about Gavin Ryng-Mayne.

Giles Ryng-Mayne?

Teddy The novelist.

Giles Oh, yes. I've vaguely heard of him. He's coming as well, is he? Splendid. What a lunch! Thank you for inviting us.

Teddy He's here for a purpose, you see. You probably know he's – no, you probably don't, why should you? – well, he's very thick within Cabinet circles. And especially thick with the Prime Minister. You see?

Giles Is he? I didn't know that . . .

Teddy Apparently writes the odd thing for them. Speeches and so on. He advises, all that. Very much behind the scenes. Occasional low profile intermediary, you know. Which is why he's coming here, actually.

Giles I see. With what purpose?

Teddy Well, they're – (*modestly*) The fact is they're intent on dragging me in, Giles. To put it bluntly, they're trying to persuade me to stand as their candidate here in the forthcoming election.

24

Giles Heavens. How exciting. Instead of Colin Theaker?

Teddy Yes. Well, Colin's been a bit of a wash-out, let's face it.

Giles Yes. Total disaster, poor man.

Teddy Nice enough chap . . .

Giles Oh, lovely man. Sweet man. Still, to be fair, Teddy, your father was a tough act to follow.

Teddy And still is. Even today. That's what's holding me back really. You know sometimes, Giles, I look back on my family, the last two generations anyway – my father, grandfather . . . I mean old Sir Ted who started it all, tough old bastard, absolute dyed in the wool fascist but say what you will about him he was a remarkable old boy. Not only started the business from scratch, built it up and ran it with a rod of iron for nearly forty years, but he was also the sitting MP for nearly twenty. I mean, that's pretty remarkable in anyone's book.

Giles Indeed. I remember he –

Teddy Then my father, Tommy Platt, he carried it all on. Turned the business international, till at one time it was the ninth biggest printers in Europe. Even today, it's the twenty-sixth biggest. Bloody amazing. And then after my grandfather had chucked it in, he also became MP for fifteen years. His is another extraordinary story.

Giles Yes, indeed. I mean, there were –

Teddy And then along comes me. If you see what I mean.

A brief silence.

(*rising*) Want a sherry or something? I was going to ask for some coffee but I feel rather like something stronger, don't you? (*Teddy goes into the dining room.*)

Giles Well, it is only quarter to nine. I'm not sure about sherry.

Teddy No, you're quite right. Hang about . . .

Giles You've done pretty well too, you know, Teddy. Don't sell yourself short.

Teddy (*from the dining room*) Think so?

Giles You've kept the business going . . .

Teddy That's about it, you see. Kept it going. Nothing new, nothing exciting. Just kept it ticking over. Now that I'm heading towards fifty, Giles, I think to myself, what have I done? Half way, well, over half way probably, and what the hell have I done with my life? (*Teddy returns with two tumblers of whisky. He hands one to Giles.*) Here you are.

Giles (*looking at it doubtfully*) Thank you.

Teddy No, when they lay me out in the family vault next to those two old monsters what are they going to write on my tombstone? Here lies Teddy Platt who more or less kept things going . . .

Giles Oh, come on . . .

Teddy Depressing thought, you know. Cheers!

Giles Cheers!

Teddy But now suddenly here's my chance. I am about to get the call.

Giles Then respond. Why not? Is this sherry?

Teddy No, it's whisky, you're quite right, far too early for sherry. No, the point is, can I do it, Giles, that's the point? Am I up to it? Will I meet the challenge? Take this country forward into the boring old millennium? Or will I just keep things going, ticking over till the right man does come along? Or woman. Sally, who knows? No, not Sally. She supports the other lot, we can't have her. But you see my dilemma?

Giles I don't think you should see it as a dilemma but as a golden opportunity which you should grasp with both hands.

Teddy You think so?

Giles I do. Indeed, I do.

Teddy Even so, you see my problem. Ryng-Mayne's here to give me the once over. Obviously he is. See if I'm up to the job. Old school friend he may be, but I haven't seen him for fifteen years. How's it going to look if my wife ignores me all through lunch? Pretends I'm not even there?

Giles (*laughing*) Well, I'm sure there are plenty of MPs' wives do that.

Teddy Yes, but not before they're elected. Most of them manage to put up some sort of a show till afterwards.

Giles Couldn't you reason with Trish? Plead with her? After all it's her future, too.

Teddy You can hardly reason with a woman who refuses to acknowledge your existence, can you?

Giles Then we'll all rally round, Teddy, don't worry. Me, Joanna . . .

Teddy Joanna?

Giles Yes, of course Joanna. She'll be happy to help. She's very fond of you both, you know that. And Sally? I know she will. And – well, as for the others, maybe they won't even notice with any luck. We can pull it off, Teddy. With a team effort we can pull it off, don't worry. Our next MP. God, this is so exciting, Teddy! Congratulations.

Teddy Now, not a word, Giles. Not yet. Top secret.

Giles Yes, of course. But so exciting.

Slight pause.

Teddy (*casually*) How is – er . . . how is old Joanna these days?

Giles Jo? (*unconvincingly*) Oh, she's . . . she's fine.

Slight pause.

No, she's not fine at all, really. I wish to God she was.

Slight pause.

The point is, I don't know quite what to do for the best, Teddy.

Teddy How do you mean?

Giles Well, you know Jo, she's – quite highly strung and – lately she's . . . she's just so up and down. Crying for no obvious reason. Getting drunk. Going for long walks on her own. I mean, we always used to walk – to walk together, but now . . . I sometimes feel she doesn't want me near her, you see . . . and I know it's me. I . . . I don't – I don't seem to – seem to – seem to be able to give her what she wants. Frankly. In any department, if you know what I mean.

Teddy Ah.

Giles I mean, if you want to know, the sex was always a bit iffy. She's not a – she's not a – she's not – God, I feel so disloyal saying this even to you – she's not a – she's not a – particularly highly sexed woman, you know.

Teddy (*a trifle surprised*) Really?

Giles Not as women – as women – go. No. Frankly, she's never really cared for it at all. Always making excuses not to – not to – or just lying there grinning and

28

bearing it, if you know what I mean. Probably me, as I say.

Teddy Well. At least she was grinning. (*He laughs rather feebly.*)

Giles With some other man she'd probably . . . It might possibly . . . Who can tell? All I know is that somewhere along the way, I feel I've let her down. Been less than the man she wanted. Whom she expected when she married. Had every right to expect. (*a fraction tearful*) She's such a terrific woman, Teddy, you've no idea. I absolutely adore her. Even after all these years.

Teddy Yes, yes . . .

Giles She's not always the easiest person, I know. But I wouldn't swap the difficulty, Teddy. I wake up some mornings, you know. She's already gone. Got up, up, up, dressed and gone out for one of her walks and I think, what would happen if one day she didn't come back to me? And you know I can't face that at all. It's like a nightmare. It's just too terrible to contemplate. I mean, you know what I mean, don't you? Don't you feel like that sometimes with Trish?

Teddy Yes, it – as I say, we're in separate rooms, I've no idea what time she gets up . . .

Giles But you know what I mean?

Teddy Yes, I know what you mean. And it's not going to happen, Giles, it certainly isn't.

Giles No?

Teddy No, old boy. Knowing you, knowing Joanna. No way.

Giles (*moved*) Thank you, Teddy, thank you for that. (*looking at him with grateful affection*) God, you'll make a wonderful MP.

Teddy (*rather moved*) Thank you.

> *A silence between them born of a deep male friendship. Trish chooses this moment to return via the terrace. She is still wearing her gardening gloves and now carries a bunch of roses as well as her secateurs. As always, she ignores Teddy, talking directly to Giles as if he was the only other person in the room.*

Trish Oh, Giles. Good. I'm glad I've caught you on your own.

Giles Sorry?

Teddy (*rising angrily*) Oh, God. Talk to her, Giles. For goodness sake talk to the woman. (*snatching the glass from Giles' hand*) I'll get us another drink. I can't stand much more of this. Sit down, both of you. (*Teddy disappears into the dining room.*)

Giles Trish . . . This is getting – well, slightly out of hand, isn't it?

Trish Giles, before you say another word, Joanna has something she needs to tell you urgently. She's in the garden.

Giles But I –

Trish Quickly. It's terribly urgent. Quickly.

Giles Yes. Of course. (*He hurries off.*)

Trish (*pleased with herself*) Good. That should clear the air. (*She goes out into the hall and closes the door.*)

Teddy (*off, from the dining room*) I don't want any more of this nonsense, Trish. I've been talking to Giles there and he's of the opinion and I'm totally in agreement with him that this is all in your mind. There's nothing medically wrong with you at all. Would you say that was a fair summary, Giles? Yes, he would. No, as far as I'm concerned, this is D-Day, Trish. D for don't bugger me about any more, just come out with whatever's on your mind and give it to me straight. I've far too much at stake here to pussy-foot. I've poured you a sherry, we're all going to sit down and talk about this like rational, civilised human beings and nobody's leaving this room, I warn you, until we've got to the bott – (*Teddy returns with two refilled glasses. Surveying the room, frustratedly*) Where the hell's everybody gone *now*? Give me strength . . .

He raises one of the glasses to his lips. As he does so, from the garden a long drawn out distant cry from Giles.

Giles (*off, distant*) Teddddddddyyyyyy!

Teddy What in the name of heaven is that?

As he stands puzzled, the lights fade to:
    Blackout.

SCENE TWO

Saturday, August 14th, 11.00 a.m.
    The same. Trish is in the dining room, now attempting the full table layout. Giles, rather irritatingly for her, follows her round like a small child. Trish sort of half listens, busying herself as they talk.

Giles (*in full flow*) . . . I mean, you can imagine the shock.

Trish (*vaguely, surveying her table*) Yes . . . yes . . .

Giles You must understand I had no inkling, Trish. None at all.

31

Trish No . . .

Giles At least you say you knew . . . Though how you could let it happen and say not a word to me, I can't imagine.

Trish Do you think it would have been helpful if I had?

Giles I think it was only proper.

Trish But the whole thing could have been over in two days, Giles, and then you'd have been none the wiser. It could have been one of those affairs, you know. The sort that if you don't know about them, you're better off not knowing . . .

Giles Has this happened to you before, Trish?

Trish Oh God, yes, masses of times. Is this her first, then? Joanna?

Giles Of course it is. (*He reflects.*) As far as I know.

Trish Exactly.

Giles So Teddy has . . . before?

Trish Oh, yes. I rather imagined he'd told you . . .

Giles Well, he made the occasional joke, but I thought they were jokes . . .

Trish I thought, you know, best friends . . .

Giles Ex-best friends, you mean.

Trish Oh, really? What a shame.

Giles What?

Trish Well, you get on so well, don't you? I think you're probably the only real friend Teddy has. I mean, nobody likes him very much, let's face it. Except that half-witted dog. Isn't there some way you could forgive and forget?

Giles After what's happened?

Trish I thought that was all part of the man thing. You know, sharing your whisky, sharing your women. Guess who I had the other night, old boy.

Giles You don't like him any more, do you? Teddy?

Trish No, not very much. Not any more. Nothing to do with this, not at all. I mean, saving your presence, I'd hardly let my marriage break up because of someone like Joanna. No, it's been a continuing thing over years, really. Like it usually is.

Giles I know you've . . . I know you've got separate – you know . . .

Trish Separate what?

Giles Bedrooms.

Trish Oh, rather. He told you that much, then? That all went very early on. I think the minute I was expecting Sally, Teddy lost complete interest. (*Slight pause.*) Well, so did I, to be perfectly honest. Whenever we made love, he always seemed in a terrible hurry to get somewhere. As if he had a train to catch. Maybe some women like it urgent. I like it to feel more like I'm on a – world cruise.

Giles What kept you together, then?

Trish Oh, God, Giles, I don't know. What keeps any marriage together? Inertia? Lack of viable alternatives? The children? I suppose sometimes if you're lucky, mutual support, deep friendship and someone you can rely on when the going gets tough. I was quite prepared to give way on the sex bit. If he needed other women, so be it – provided they weren't close friends of mine and he didn't bring them home like a cat and leave them on the doormat, I didn't mind. But it was the other bit really. That's when I stopped loving him. When

33

I realised that I could no longer trust him as a friend; no longer rely on him to stand by me – when things got difficult . . . You see?

Giles No chance of – bridge building?

Trish It's not a river between us any more, Giles. It's an ocean.

Giles Oh, dear. How sad. How very sad. Sometimes, you know, Trish, just sitting down and talking it out between you, it can really –

Trish Giles. Thanks awfully for the advice. I'm really most touched and grateful, but don't you think that you should be sorting out your own marriage . . .?

Giles Oh. I am – I am so – so sorry.

Trish No, don't take that the wrong way, I just –

Giles No, no, you're quite right I have no – I've no – it's just that other people's problems always appear somehow simpler, don't they?

Trish They seem simpler, anyway. Though, in the case of Joanna, maybe . . .

Giles She's a – rather unusual person.

Trish Yes?

Giles I – I still love her enormously, you know.

Trish Good.

Giles I can't help thinking that – having done what she's – she's – she's – done – I should – I should – I should look a bit to myself. I mean, the guilt's never just one – one – one-sided, is it?

Trish Usually not. In my case it is. But usually not.

Giles Cast out the – beam in thine own eye, eh? I won't disturb you any more, Trish. Thank you for – thank you for –

Trish Why don't you go home and talk to her, Giles?

Giles I'll try. It's not – she's a bit – funny thing, guilt.

Trish (*unconvinced*) Yes. See you both for lunch, then.

Giles Oh. You'd still welcome us here, would you? At your table?

Trish I certainly would. I've just worked out these bloody place settings. Don't you dare let me down, either of you. Too late to ask anyone else.

Giles I don't know what I'm going to say to Teddy, I'm sure.

Trish If you can't think of anything, do what I do. Ignore him.

Giles It may come to that. I'll be off, then. Start the peace process.

Trish Giles . . .

Giles Mmmm?

Trish I know it's shared responsibility and all that but – do remember it was Joanna who had the affair, not you . . .

Giles Yes, of course . . . Have to talk to Jake as well, I suppose. I don't know how he's going to take it, poor lad. He's so – trusting.

Giles goes out through the French windows. Izzie comes in with some plates of cocktail nibbles on a tray.

Izzie I'm laying out the nibbles in here then, Patricia.

Trish Right-o, Izzie.

Izzie That French woman's driver just telephoned. They're running half an hour behind down the motorway.

Trish Oh, dear.

Izzie I'll hold back lunch, shall I?

Trish If you can.

Izzie I won't be responsible, mark you. You should never have ordered beef.

Trish No, you were quite right, Izzie . . .

Izzie You'll rue the day . . .

Trish (*calling*) Has Pearl vacuumed in here yet, Izzie?

Izzie Probably not, knowing her.

Trish Doesn't look as if she has. There's bits all over this floor. She should have done it before we laid the table.

Izzie She needs boiling in oil and then strangling, that girl.

Trish Can you call her and tell her to do it at once, Izzie? Before people start arriving. Leave those for now . . .

Izzie Right.

Izzie goes out, leaving the tray half unloaded on the sofa. Teddy comes in from the hall. He has now dressed for lunch. He stops in the doorway, hears Trish in the dining room and moves to the double doors.

Teddy Ah, there you are. Good. Right. Trish, it's time for straight talk.

*Trish ignores him as usual, continuing to lay her
dining table.*

Yes, alright, carry on doing that if you have to. You
don't even have to speak, if you prefer, but I do want
you to listen, Trish. Because what I have to say is vitally
important. OK?

*No response. During the next, as he warms to his
address, Teddy moves away from the doorway and
paces the sitting room. At some stage, Trish leaves the
dining room by the offstage door. Teddy remains
unaware of this and continues to address the empty
dining room.*

Well, I'll have to take it on trust that you're listening,
I suppose. Look, Trish, this cannot go on, this silence
between us – this one-sided silence, that is. I'm not silent.
I'm not the silent one, am I? I'm happy to talk. I'll talk
all day. It's you and this ridiculous . . . I mean, if you'd
only explain to me what the problem is, we could sort it
out. But you're not giving me the chance, are you? That's
the point, old thing. I mean, it can't be this Joanna
business surely? I mean, that was . . . well, you know
what that was. Of course you do. Bit of mutual nooky,
that's all that was. Nothing on either side. But as soon
as I – suspected that was affecting you – the minute
I did – well, I jacked it in. I said to her, it can't go on,
sorry. It's upsetting Trish. The last thing I ever want is
for you to be upset. I mean, you're number one, Trish.
You're the first officer. I mean, Joanna was just a –
midshipman. AB two. Whatever they call them.

*Trish has gone. Unseen by Teddy, Pearl comes into
the dining room also via the far door. She carries the
vacuum cleaner. She plugs it in but stands just inside
the doors, poised to start, waiting for Teddy to stop
speaking.*

37

The point is today is crunch day, Trish. I can't say too much – not just at present because it's all very hush-hush. Nobody must know about this, not a soul. But. The reason Gavin Ryng-Mayne is here is to make me an offer. I can't be any more precise but let's just say we might be looking very shortly for a little pied-à-terre in Westminster. OK? 'Nough said? Now it's vital we impress this chap. He's an old school friend so he's on our side. Just pull out all the stops, there's a good girl. Laugh at the jokes, I know you've heard them a million times but – tell him I'm sliced Hovis – you know, all the usual rubbish. I don't have to tell you, I – Listen, the – our sleeping arrangements, Trish. I was having a chat with – I was having a think – and I wondered if we should try it on the same mattress for a bit. Just to see if we could – I mean, it's been some time, I know – it's been, well, about seventeen years, hasn't it – so we may be a bit – you may be feeling a bit rusty, you know. But I'm prepared to give it a whirl. Crack open a bottle of bubbly. Root out the frilly night wear, you know . . . all that rubbish . . . How do you feel?

He comes face to face with Pearl.

Pearl Fine by me . . .

Teddy (*furiously*) Oh, for the love of – where's my bloody wife?

Pearl I dunno. Upstairs I think.

Teddy How much of that were you listening to? How much of that did you hear?

Pearl All of it.

Teddy Well, get on with your work. You've no business eavesdropping at doors. That was a private conversation between my wife and myself.

Pearl She's not here.

Teddy That is entirely beside the point. Whether she is here or not has nothing at all to do with it. Get on with your work at once, do you hear?

Pearl (*unaffected by this*) Right.

Pearl closes the double doors. Teddy stamps about furiously.

Teddy The whole of my future at stake and the woman isn't even prepared to listen. Well, to hell with her. I'll manage on my own.

He sits on the tray of canapés on the sofa. Izzie comes in with a tray of sherry.

Oh, shit! For crying out loud. Who put these on there? These are new trousers. Now look at them. Did you put these on there?

Izzie I was called away.

Teddy Bloody stupid thing to do. Have you got a damp cloth?

Izzie Not on me.

Teddy Well, where?

Izzie In the kitchen. I didn't know you were going to sit on 'em, did I? Ruined now, those are.

Teddy I have a very important meeting this morning, I hope you appreciate that. With a very, very important man.

Izzie Hope he doesn't like rare beef.

Teddy A top secret meeting. So I want everything done properly, do you hear?

Izzie I can't keep taking it in and out, you know . . .

Teddy You just behave yourself. In a few months you could find yourself having to vote for me . . .

Izzie goes out through the hall door, taking the tray and the spoiled canapés with her. Teddy stamps about looking for a cloth. He finally goes into the dining room, takes one of Trish's carefully folded napkins off the table and, unfolding it, starts to try to clean the seat of his trousers with that. He is performing this somewhat convoluted dance when Gavin is shown in through the French windows by Sally. Gavin is in his late forties, urbane, charming and attractive, the ideal diplomat.

Sally If you'd like to wait in here, I'll see if I can find anyone.

Gavin (*smiling at her warmly*) Thank you, Sally. See you later.

Sally goes off along the terrace. Gavin enters the apparently empty room and, hearing Teddy's efforts from the dining room, cautiously investigates.

Gavin (*seeing Teddy*) Ah! There he is!

Teddy (*hastily stopping his current activity*) Aha!

Gavin Teddy! Dear, dear fellow.

Teddy (*waving the napkin in greeting*) Gavin! Dear chap!

They embrace.

How good to see you, Sparky. Haven't changed a scrap.

Gavin Nor you, nor you . . . And you know, seeing Sally again just now, it made me realise how long it's been. I mean, she was tiny – six months, something like that – when I last saw her . . .

Teddy That long ago, was it . . .?

40

Gavin If you remember, I was very nearly her godfather.

Teddy Yes, of course – excuse me, got some vol au vent on my trousers – yes, of course you were . . . (*Teddy tosses the napkin back into the dining room and closes the doors.*)

Gavin I was trying to remember on the way here. I only met Trish the once, I think. That was at that old school do.

Teddy Oh God, yes. Years ago. At the Savoy. Old Boys' dance. Fund raising.

Gavin You got it. (*taking in the room*) Oh, just look at this! Look at this! Isn't this wonderful? What a pad, Teddy. What would this place be? Seventeen – what? 1770, 1780?

Teddy 1753.

Gavin Oh, really? That early?

In the dining room, Pearl starts vacuuming noisily.

Teddy Well, the original house was Tudor. Early Tudor – (*registering the noise*) – what is going on in there? – but my great, great, great, great, great whatever – Edward Platt – he succeeded in burning the place to the ground –

Gavin Oh, dear . . .

Teddy Which apparently started as a row with his wife. Only it got a bit out of hand.

Gavin Heavens!

Teddy And his wife –

Next door, the vacuum bumps and bangs.

– what is she doing? – his wife unfortunately died in the fire, poor woman, along with about nine of their

41

children and subsequently he built the present house in their memory –

Gavin Nice gesture . . .

Teddy Which, as you say, was a nice gesture. And he was subsequently killed in a hunting accident and the estate passed to the second son –

Gavin Second *surviving* son, presumably . . .

Teddy Quite. The first son, Thomas Platt, was put away because he was completely barking. And the second son, Edward . . .

The vacuum cleaner now starts banging against the double doors.

And the second son, also called Edward – Oh, for God's sake, this is just too much, excuse me –

Teddy goes to the double doors and flings them open. Pearl is revealed in mid-vacuum.

(*angrily*) What are you doing?

Pearl What?

Teddy Switch it off.

Pearl strains to hear him.

SWITCH IT OFF!

Pearl switches off.

Pearl I was told to vacuum.

Teddy Not now.

Pearl Mrs Platt told me to vacuum.

Teddy Well, I'm telling you not to. Go and vacuum somewhere else.

Pearl (*affably*) Righty-o. (*to Gavin*) 'Morning.

Gavin (*charmingly*) Good morning.

Pearl It's staying fine at the moment, anyway. Any luck, it'll stay this way for the fête this afftern –

Teddy shuts the doors on her in mid-sentence.

Teddy And the second son, Edward Platt – they're all called Edward or Thomas, it's very confusing . . . He was apparently quite a bright chap who finished the place off by building the West Wing – what we still call the new wing, although these days it's actually the oldest bit of the building –

Gavin What part are we in now?

Teddy This? This is the old library. Actually built in 1850. But although it's called the old library, it actually replaced the previous library which was much, much older and eventually fell down. But although this was called the old library, curiously enough it was never used as a library. It was built by Thomas Platt for his new young bride as a wedding gift. But on their honeymoon cruise the poor girl fell overboard and as a result this room was never finished. In fact he had it boarded up. And consequently it wasn't used for thirty years and there's hardly been a book in here since.

Gavin What a waste.

Teddy In fact, it was eventually opened up again by my great-grandfather, Tom Platt. Old Tom Platt. His wife Catherine sadly died of food poisoning and he opened it up as a memorial to her. That's her picture up there, you see. That's old Cat Platt as she's generally known.

Gavin Oh, yes.

Teddy She's no oil painting, I'm afraid. But I think he's caught the dog rather well.

Gavin Yes, indeed.

Teddy And that's about it. We had the bomb, of course. German. During the war. That took care of the East Wing. Don't know what the hell they were trying to hit . . . Anyway, I'm afraid they did hit my grandmother, who'd taken up residence there after my grandfather, Ted Platt, died which was very sad for everybody, of course, because she was a deeply wonderful rich character.

Gavin Yes. On the whole they've not had a lot of luck, have they? The women in your family?

Teddy No, it's perfectly true. What was it my father used to say? Marry a Platt and that's that. (*He laughs.*)

Gavin (*laughing*) No, it's wonderful to have such a family history, though. Must give you a great sense of permanence.

Teddy Yes, I suppose it does.

Gavin I do envy that.

Teddy You don't go back then?

Gavin Well, yes, we do go back. But in assorted directions.

Teddy Ah.

Gavin Welsh.

Teddy Really.

Gavin Turkish.

Teddy Good Lord.

Gavin I understand Portuguese Jewish . . .

Teddy Grief. I never knew this, Sparky.

Gavin And just a dash of Irish on my mother's side. Quite a mongrel.

Teddy (*laughing*) Gets a bit crowded at Christmas, I imagine.

Gavin No. (*rather sadly*) No, no.

Teddy Well, I never knew that about you. All these years.

Gavin I think at our particular school, at that time it was prudent to keep a fairly low profile about mixed parentage . . .

Teddy Yes.

Gavin All changed now, of course.

Teddy Oh, yes. Girls as well now.

Gavin Yes. They'd have been a bonus in our day, wouldn't they? Still we managed, didn't we?

Teddy Yes. (*changing the subject*) God, it's good to see you again, Sparky.

> *As they reflect on this, Trish enters.*
> *Gavin springs to his feet. Teddy tardily follows suit.*
> *As always, Trish ignores Teddy.*

Trish (*extending her hand to Gavin*) Hallo, there. I'm so sorry I wasn't here to greet you.

Gavin How do you do?

Trish I don't know if you'll remember me. I'm Patricia . . .

Gavin Trish. Yes, of course, how could I forget? Gavin Ryng-Mayne with a Y. Gavin, please. I was just hearing about your –

Trish I'm so sorry, you've been left all on your own, that's terrible. I'll see if I can find my husband, he's around somewhere. Would you excuse me, I won't be one second, then we can have a sherry.

45

Gavin I – er . . .

A crash of a plate breaking in the dining room.

Trish (*hearing this*) Excuse me. (*She opens the dining room doors.*) Pearl, what are you doing?

Pearl (*off*) I was just dusting . . .

Trish Well, don't dust the dining table, girl. We're just about to eat off it. (*to Gavin*) Do excuse me.

Trish closes the doors behind her.
  Gavin, totally bemused, looks at Teddy.
  Teddy, after a second, decides the best course is to laugh it off. He does.

Teddy (*laughing*) Trish! She's legendary. Absolutely legendary.

Gavin Is she?

Teddy Absolutely. Well known.

Gavin I don't quite follow.

Teddy Trish's sense of humour . . . famous throughout the county . . .

Gavin Indeed?

Teddy It's – it takes a bit of getting used to. It's a bit of an acquired taste . . . but once you're on her wavelength . . .

Gavin Yes?

Teddy Great practical joker, too . . .

Gavin Is she?

Teddy Thank your lucky stars you're not staying the night.

Gavin Yes?

Teddy Wake up with a hedgehog in your bed. (*He laughs.*)

Gavin laughs, too, but still looks a little uncertain.

Anyway. To business. À nos moutons, as our French guest would probably put it. Incidentally, we've got a French film actress coming for lunch, by the way. She's coming to open our annual fête down in the garden there.

Gavin Yes, I saw some activity when I was . . .

Teddy I don't know what films she's been in. Apparently, in her recent one she gets blown up early on.

Gavin Sounds like one of your family . . .

Teddy (*laughing heartily*) Yes. But everyone says she's very good indeed. I'm afraid I haven't seen it. Still, she should liven it up. Hope she speaks English because she's not going to get much out of us otherwise. Now.

Gavin Yes. Well, you know why I'm here. I'm sure you do. We need you, Teddy. It's as simple as that. As you know, I'm fairly close to the PM and we had a private dinner party the other night – just three or four of us – Chris Baxendale . . .

Teddy Yes . . .

Gavin . . . Simon Wickstead . . . Charlie Havers . . .

Teddy . . . yes, yes . . .

Gavin . . . Rowena Todd-Martin . . .

Teddy No, I don't know her . . .

Gavin Rowena? Well, in that rarefied circle, let's just say she's big. She's very, very big. And she's going to get bigger.

Teddy Really?

Gavin There are plans for her. Believe me. Anyway. What we've got with this constituency, Teddy, is a seat that's rapidly slipping from under us. At the next election, it could well turn. I'm sure you're aware of that. I mean Theaker's not the right stuff, he really isn't. Nice enough man . . .

Teddy Oh, yes, very very nice man . . .

Gavin But he's not cutting it and we can't afford to pay his keep. Cruel facts. But these days, politics is a cut-throat business, Teddy. And we're turning to you, cap in hand. Third generation of Platts. Your family made the seat practically a family business, you could easily have taken it on after your father stood down. But you chose, perhaps wisely at the time, not to.

Teddy Well, there was the business, of course.

Gavin Of course, there was the business, we all appreciated that. But as I understand it, these days you're involved slightly less . . .

Teddy Slightly less, yes . . .

Gavin So we're appealing to you. I'm, of course, just the intermediary. But I do speak for the PM. He wants you to know – and I quote his exact words on this – he wants you to know he would be forever in your debt.

Teddy I see. I see.

Gavin (*slowly*) For – ever – in – your – debt.

    Teddy nods.

Yes? Need I say more?

Teddy He'd like me to stand?

Gavin He would.

Teddy At the next election?

Gavin Yes.

Teddy Well, they'd have to pick me first – select me – whatever they do, wouldn't they?

Gavin That's all taken care of. Don't worry.

Teddy Really? What about Colin Theaker? Where does he stand?

Gavin He doesn't. Let's say he's – seen the axe and bowed his head to the inevitable.

Teddy (*filled with regret*) He's such a nice man.

Gavin Charming man. Charming. (*laughing*) Too nice for politics. Well?

Teddy The thing is, I want to say yes to you, Sparky. I hear what you're saying and I can see where you're coming from and I want more than anything else to say yes. The question, you see, I keep asking myself is – do I need it?

Gavin Teddy, let me put it this way. You can do perfectly well without this government but ask yourself this, can this government do without you?

Teddy Yes. I see. Put like that . . .

Gavin I think the PM's gratitude is not to be dismissed lightly. There are one or two little perks that could quite easily come your way . . .

Teddy You mean, ministerial office . . .?

Gavin (*who wasn't meaning this at all*) Yes . . . eventually . . . that as well. But I think he's pretty happy with the team at present. I mean, there might be some temporary very, very minor post, Arts Minister, something like that – but, no, there are a lot of select committees and commissions, Teddy. POI's as we call them . . .

Teddy POI's?

Gavin Putting Off the Inevitables. Quite high profile, some of them. For instance, he gave me permission to mention the forthcoming Enquiry into the Moral Conduct of Members, which is quite a hot potato, you can imagine. They are looking for someone to chair that, someone who's absolutely squeaky clean. That's vital, as you appreciate.

Teddy Absolutely.

Gavin The trouble is finding anyone who'll stand up to that sort of scrutiny. The sort of scrutiny that those bastards are going to put them under.

Teddy The committee?

Gavin No, the press. I mean, whoever serves on that committee better wear their rubber pants. Because they'll be swarming all over them.

Teddy (*a little worried*) I see.

Gavin But then which one of us is blameless? (*in a slightly dodgy Scots accent*)
'Morality, thou deadly bane,
Thy tens o' thousands thou hast slain!'

Teddy Very, very true.

Gavin Rabbie Burns . . .

Teddy (*nodding gravely*) Especially these days.

Gavin Anyway. What do you say, matey?

Teddy Well, I think I'm bound to say yes, aren't I?

Gavin Then it's yes?

Teddy Looks like it.

Gavin I can tell the PM you've accepted?

Teddy Yes, you can.

Gavin He'll be overjoyed. I'll phone him after lunch. I have his private number.

Teddy Where is he? Chequers?

Gavin Eastbourne.

Teddy (*laughing*) What's he doing there? Dirty weekend?

Gavin Conference.

Teddy Oh yes, of course. Sorry. Listen, can I offer you a sherry? While we're waiting for the others? Whisky, perhaps?

Gavin Sherry, thank you. That would be very nice.

Teddy (*as he pours two glasses*) Incidentally, talking of morals, I was upset to read all that rubbish about you a year or so back.

Gavin Oh, that. We soon settled that, don't worry. Cost them a packet, too.

Teddy Good for you. Under-age, wasn't she? Something of the sort?

Gavin Yes, she was under age. She was fifteen and a half. I found the girl on my doorstep distributing Christian literature, she was absolutely soaked, she'd got caught in the rain, I invited her inside and gave her some dry clothes. End of story. Someone gets hold of it. Blows it up out of all proportion. (*taking the glass*) Cheers.

Teddy Bastards, aren't they? Bastards. I don't know why they publish that sort of filth. I mean, who the hell's interested?

Gavin God knows. Just be warned, Teddy. If you're coming into this line, keep your shirt tucked in. Here's to you.

Teddy Cheers, Sparky!

Gavin Incidentally, I'm not known all that often as Sparky. Not these days.

Teddy Oh, fair enough.

Gavin But then I don't suppose many people call you Penelope, do they?

Teddy No, no. Thank God.

Gavin Incidentally, we must keep all this quiet for a day or two. At least till all the right people have been notified.

Teddy Such as Colin Theaker?

Gavin Yes, Colin Theaker, obviously. I think the Prime Minister will probably want a personal word with him.

Teddy Poor chap.

Gavin Yes.

Trish enters.

Trish No, I'm sorry, Gavin, I can't find Teddy anywhere. Don't know where he's gone.

Teddy laughs. Gavin laughs a little forcedly.

He'll roll up eventually, I expect. Oh, you've helped yourself to sherry. Jolly sensible. I think I'll join you. (*as she pours herself a glass*) Now, we've just heard that their car's turned into the village, so Madame Cadeau plus her driver should be with us any minute. Lucille Cadeau. I don't know if you've heard of her. She's a French film star.

52

Teddy Yes, I've just told him, Trish . . .

Trish Have you heard of her, at all?

Gavin I hadn't, but –

Teddy I've told him, she's coming to open our fête . . .

Trish She's here to open our garden fête this afternoon.

Gavin Really?

Teddy I've told him that already, Trish . . .

Trish Now, who else have we got coming? Oh, two very special friends of ours, Giles and Joanna Mace. Well, they're our closest neighbours actually. They live just at the bottom of our garden.

Teddy Giles is our local doctor . . .

Trish Giles is the village doctor . . .

Gavin Oh, yes . . .?

Teddy And Joanna's a teacher . . .

Trish And Joanna teaches . . .

Gavin Locally?

Trish What?

Teddy What?

Gavin Locally? Does she teach locally?

Trish Oh, yes . . .

Teddy Yes. Up at Sally's school, actually . . .

Trish Up at our daughter Sally's school. Only Joanna teaches the juniors.

Teddy The juniors.

Gavin Yes.

53

Silence.
    Teddy laughs, unconvincingly.
    Silence.

Do you – ?

Teddy (*together*) Sorry?

Trish (*together*) Sorry?

Gavin Nothing.

    Giles and Joanna appear on the terrace. They both,
    too, have chosen to ignore Teddy.

Teddy (*seeing them, with some relief*) Ah, here they
are . . .

Trish (*seeing them*) Oh, talk of the devil . . .

Teddy Come in, come in . . .

Joanna (*very tense*) May we come in?

Trish Yes, do. Come and meet Gavin. Gavin, this is Jo,
Joanna Mace, a very old friend of ours. And this is Giles.

Gavin How do you do? Gavin Ryng-Mayne. With a Y.

Joanna With a what?

Gavin With a Y.

Joanna Why what?

Gavin That's how it's spelt. With a Y.

Joanna Oh, I see. With a Y.

Giles Hallo. Giles Mace, how do you do?

Teddy Would you both care for a sherry?

Joanna (*to Gavin*) Did you drive down this morning?

Gavin Yes, I did. I started quite early . . .

Teddy Sherry, both of you?

Giles How long did that take you?

Gavin I think almost exactly three hours.

Teddy Do either of you want a bloody sherry, yes or no?

Trish That's terribly good going.

Giles You must have been travelling.

Gavin I think I was just a wee bit the far side of the speed limit.

Trish Now, would you both like a glass of sherry?

Joanna Lovely.

Giles Thank you.

Teddy The fastest I ever did it from London, you know –

Giles What do you drive?

Gavin A little Porsche.

Joanna Golly.

Gavin Just a small one.

Teddy You know, the fastest I ever did it from London . . .

Trish (*handing out the sherry glasses*) Here we are. Jo?

Joanna Oh, thank you.

Teddy The fastest –

Trish Giles?

Giles Thank you so much.

Teddy The fastest time I ever did it –

Giles I'm looking forward to meeting our film star . . .

Teddy – in the middle of the day –

Trish Oh, yes. Exciting, isn't it?

Teddy – was two hours –

Trish That reminds me. I must keep an eye out for them. We don't want them going round to the back like you did, Gavin.

Teddy – two hours – and forty-six minutes –

Trish Our gardener's removed all the signs for some reason.

Teddy – door to fucking door.

Gavin Why did he do that?

Trish Don't ask me, he's a law unto himself . . .

Teddy What about that then, you stupid bastards? (*to Gavin*) Sorry.

Sally comes in from the hall. She has changed for lunch out of her school clothes.

Trish Oh, Sally, you haven't seen your father, have you?

Sally No. Mum, they're here. They've arrived. Pearl's just seen their car.

Trish Oh, heavens. Why don't we all go and meet her? Wouldn't that be fun? We can all cheer. She'll think she's at Cannes. You all coming? (*She starts for the hall.*)

Joanna (*following her*) Oh, yes. Let's go and meet her.

Giles (*following them*) Why not?

Gavin (*following them*) Good idea.

Sally (*going with them*) She's somewhere round the front . . .

They have all gone, apart from Teddy.
He glares after them.

From the dining room, a crash. Teddy crosses and opens the door. Pearl is standing there.

Teddy What are you doing?

Pearl I dropped one of them fish pasties.

Teddy Well, then scrape it up.

Pearl I'm going to.

Teddy shuts the door on her. He decides this is the moment to rehearse his acceptance speech.

Teddy (*clearing his throat*) Ladies and gentlemen . . . er – fellow party members . . . Prime Minister . . . er – no, minister . . . junior minister . . . whoever you are . . . this is a very, very great . . . this is an extremely . . . huge honour . . . to be your new MP . . . and I can promise you right here and now that I intend fully to carry this fight to the opposition and I shall not cease until I personally see the whites of their eyes as they turn tail and run . . . the seats of their pants as they turn tail and run! I stand before you today – this evening – your sitting member . . . (*He thinks about this.*) . . . I sit here your standing mem – no, no, no . . . your fully erected member – oh, bloody hell – your elected representative . . . and I can promise you that your vote for me has meant a vote for sanity, a vote for humanity, a vote for . . . (*He runs through a few rhyming options.*) . . . banity, canity . . . danity, hanity, inanity? . . . no . . . vanity . . . yanity . . . zanity . . . and a vote for good old-fashioned common sense. So, as my great uncle Eddie, huntsman and bon viveur, was wont to say, get off your ass, spread your legs, get mounted and get at 'em! Tally-ho and God speed!

As he finishes, Lucille appears at the French windows. She is everything expected of a French film star, attractive, vivacious and charming.

Teddy turns and sees her. He gawps. If there is such a thing as love at first sight, this is it.

Teddy Ah.

Lucille Ah. Pardon. Sorry . . . we have come . . . wrong . . .

Teddy (*who believes the best way to converse with foreigners is to shout at them*) Ah. Tu es . . . vous êtes . . . Madame Cadeau?

Lucille I am Lucille. You . . . are . . . Mr Plate?

Teddy Platt. Teddy. I am Teddy. I am named Teddy.

Lucille Ah. So. Teddy.

Fran, Lucille's driver, appears on the terrace behind her. She seems fairly formidable.

Oh. This . . . my driver. Fran.

Teddy Fran? Ah. Welcome also . . . here. I am welcoming you . . .

Fran (*in a flat London voice*) It's alright. I speak English.

Teddy Oh, splendid. Please, do come in. Entrez! I'm afraid you'll find . . . here . . . very few of us . . . speaking the French. Je regrette. Rien de français.

* **Lucille** (*shrugging*) Oh, c'est pas grave. J'ai l'habitude. Quand on travaille souvent en Angleterre ou en Amérique on s'aperçoit que très peu de gens parlent français. Bien sûr, je devrais apprendre l'anglais, mais j'ai si peu de temps. Et je suis aussi très paresseuse . . .

Teddy Yes. Jolly good. We find that, too. Especially during the summer.

---

* Oh, it doesn't matter. I'm used to that. If you work a lot in England or America you find very few people speak French. I should learn English, of course, but I have so little time. I'm also very lazy . . .

At this moment, through the hall doors the others return, led by Trish.

Trish Oh, you're here. Hallo.

All Hallo!

Teddy Ah, everybody. This is Lucille. I'm afraid she doesn't speak much English so we'll have to be . . .

Lucille Hallo. I – come in the wrong door. I speak not good English, so . . . I'm afraid.

* **Trish** Alors nous allons parler français. (*to the others*) We'll all have to speak French, won't we? (*plunging into fluent French*) Bienvenue, Madame Cadeau, c'est gentil de votre part de nous consacrer un peu de votre temps si précieux . . .

Lucille Oh, mais tout le plaisir est pour moi. C'est tellement plus agréable d'être dans la campagne anglaise plutôt qu'enfermée dans des chambres d'hotel . . . C'est si beau . . .

Giles Vous avez fait bon voyage? On m'a dit que vous avez été retardée sur l'autoroute . . .

Lucille C'était épouvantable, la circulation était épouvantable . . .

Fran Il y avait une foire agricole. La route était pleine de tracteurs . . .

---

* **Trish** Then we'll speak French. (*to the others*) We'll all have to speak French, won't we? (*plunging into fluent French*) Welcome, Madame Cadeau, it's so good of you to give up your valuable time . . .

Lucille Oh, it's a pleasure. It's so good to see the English countryside instead of hotel rooms . . . It's so beautiful . . .

Giles How was your journey? I hear you were held up on the motorway . . .

Lucille It was bad, the traffic was very bad . . .

Fran There was some agricultural show on. The road was full of tractors . . .

* **Giles** Oh, vous n'auriez pas dû prendre cette route. Pas aujourd'hui. C'est le jour du 'County Show'.

Fran J'ai utilisé la carte qu'on m'a donnée au studio. Ils n'ont pas parlé d'une foire.

Joanna (*simultaneously with the last*) C'est la première fois que vous voyagez en dehors de Londres?

Lucille Oui, la première fois, j'ai honte de le dire . . .

Sally Eh bien alors, vous n'avez pas encore vu ce qu'il y a de mieux à voir.

Trish Je suppose que c'est ça le problème quand on fait des films, hein? On est toujours cloîtré à l'intérieur, n'est ce pas?

Sally Oh, maman, écoute, on n'est pas toujours enfermé. Maintenant la plupart des films sont faits en extérieur . . .

Gavin (*simultaneously over this last, to Lucille*) Dites-moi, est-ce-que vous trouvez qu'il y a une grosse différence entre faire des films en Angleterre et faire des films en France?

---

* **Giles** Oh, you shouldn't have come that way. Not today. It's the day of the County Show.

Fran I used the map the studio gave me. They said nothing about a show.

Joanna (*simultaneously with the last*) Is this the first time you've travelled out of London?

Lucille Yes, it is, I'm ashamed to say . . .

Sally Oh, well, you've not seen the best of the place, then.

Trish I suppose that's the trouble with making movies, isn't it? You're always cooped up indoors, aren't you?

Sally Oh, Mum, honestly, they're not always indoors. Most of the films these days are made on location . . .

Gavin (*simultaneously over this last, to Lucille*) Tell me, do you find it very different making movies in England as opposed to making movies in France?

* **Lucille** Eh! Un film est un film est un film. Non, mais c'est vrai il y a des différences. Surtout en ce qui concerne les studios. Les studios d'Hollywood sont énormes, en gros bien plus grands que nos studios en Europe . . .

> *They all crowd together and chatter happily in a babble of French. Teddy finds himself on the edge of the group, isolated and alone.*

Teddy (*frustratedly*) Oh, for God's sake. Doesn't anybody here speak English?

> *The chatter continues as the lights fade to:*
> *Blackout.*

---

* Well, a film is a film is a film. But yes, there are differences. Mainly in the set up of the studios themselves. Hollywood studios are very big, of course, far bigger than we have in Europe, on the whole . . .

Act Two

SCENE ONE

Saturday, August 14th, 2.00 p.m.
   The same.
   Lunch is just about over. In the sitting room are Trish, Sally and Gavin, finishing their coffee. Sally also has a glass of red wine. In the dining room, through the half open door, the sound and the occasional glimpse of Teddy and Lucille, who've obviously hit it off despite the language difficulty. The two alternate between a low murmur and sudden bellows of laughter. Teddy has clearly had several drinks over lunch. Joanna and Giles have left.

Gavin What a simply delicious lunch. Thank you so much.

Trish Yes. Izzie usually gets her beef rather rarer than that, I'm so sorry.

   A roar of laughter from the dining room. Trish frowns slightly.

Gavin No, no, actually I prefer it on the – well-done side.

Sally (*lightly drunk*) It was as tough as old wellingtons …

Trish I mean, it was very silly of me to choose sirloin but I thought it would be rather nice for our French guest. You know, roast beef of old England.

Sally Roast boot of old England, you mean …

Gavin I'm sure Lucille appreciated it.

Trish Are your trousers quite dry now?

Gavin Yes, absolutely fine. Nothing serious.

Trish She's such a clumsy girl. When she's not breaking crockery she's pouring water over people.

Another laugh from the dining room.

I must ask her to do up more buttons in future as well.

Gavin Well. I'd certainly no objection to that. (*He laughs.*)

Trish No, but – all the same. It's – I'm sure it's unhygienic. I mean, Giles practically had his nose wedged in there at one point. Incidentally, I must apologise for our friends rushing off in the middle of the meal like that. Joanna had this important overseas phone call, apparently. And Giles had to . . . had to . . .

Gavin Had to go and hold the receiver for her. (*He laughs.*) Still, more wine for us, eh?

Trish Helped to wash down the beef, anyway.

Sally The fillet of beef Wellington . . .

Trish Yes, don't keep on, darling. How many glasses of that have you had?

Sally Two. This is my second, that's all . . .

Trish You've certainly –

More laughter from the dining room.

(*getting up*) Excuse me . . . (*She closes the dining room doors.*)

Sally (*to Gavin*) Two glasses of wine, I'm some sort of alcoholic.

Trish You've had more than two.

Sally How do you know?

Trish Because I've been counting.

Sally You've been sitting there counting the number of glasses I've had? (*to Gavin*) Wouldn't you consider that slightly over-protective? I mean, wouldn't you?

Gavin (*reluctant to be drawn*) Well . . .

Sally Anyway, red wine's good for you. There's been fresh research recently –

Trish I don't care, it's still not good for you to drink too much.

Gavin I don't blame you. It's a stunning claret. Absolutely clock-stopping.

Trish I don't care, she shouldn't drink too much of it. Apart from anything else, by the time you're forty you'll be a red-faced, fat, boring drunk.

Pearl has entered from the hall.

Yes, Pearl?

Pearl I done the dishes. I'll be off now.

Trish Yes, alright, Pearl.

Pearl Got to get ready for my fortune-telling down in my little tent. (*winking at Gavin*) Your trousers alright, are they?

Gavin Yes, thank you.

Pearl Sorry about that. Hope nothing's shrunk . . .

Trish You've put everything away as well, have you, Pearl?

Pearl Oh, yes.

Trish No more breakages, I hope?

Pearl Oh, no. (*as she goes*) Not so's you'd notice. (*Pearl goes.*)

Trish (*sighing*) Excuse me, I'd better go and see what damage she's done. (*Trish opens the dining room doors.*)
* Je voulais seulement vous rappeler que c'est presque l'heure de la cérémomie d'ouverture, Lucille . . .

Lucille Ah, oui, merci.

Teddy I've been introducing Lucille to the joys of single malt whi –

>   *Trish closes the doors on Teddy in mid-sentence. She goes out of the hall door.*

Sally You're a – what do you call it – you're a wine buff then, are you?

Gavin Lord, no. I have a working knowledge of one or two favourites. I can tell a good one from el plonko.

Sally Is this a good one?

Gavin Very good. Can't you tell?

Sally Wine's wine to me . . .

Gavin (*smiling*) I don't believe that for a moment.

Sally What is it then? Tell me about it. It's a claret, is it?

Gavin Yes, it's a Bordeaux.

Sally Is that good?

Gavin Not of itself. That's just the generic name. It's a Saint-Julien from the district of Haut-Medoc. Which is one of the most famous of the French wine growing regions. Which includes Margaux, Pauillac, Saint-Julien . . . What

---

* Just to remind you, it's nearly time for the opening ceremony, Lucille . . .

Lucille Ah, yes. Thank you.

65

you're drinking there is a Château Leoville-Barton which is certainly one of the best. It's a second growth, what they term a deuxième cru which is pretty high up the league table – there are some who think it ought to be ranked higher – but what makes that particularly special is that it's a '71 and you can't do much better than that.

Sally 1971. Before I was born.

Gavin Long before.

Sally How old would you have been? In 1971?

Gavin Considerably younger than I am now.

Sally You're not going to tell me?

Gavin No.

Sally I told you my age.

Gavin That's different. It's very good to be your age.

Sally I don't think it is.

Gavin No?

Sally When you're my age you still tend to get treated like a child.

Gavin Only by your parents, surely? And they can't help that, can they, poor things?

Sally You don't look on me as a child, then?

Gavin No. I don't look on you as a child, not at all.

A silence as they stare at each other.

Sally (*holding out her glass, a little coquettish*) Want a sip?

Gavin No, thank you. I'm afraid I can't take it these days. Not at my age.

Sally I don't believe that for a moment.

Jake has appeared on the terrace.

(*half to herself*) Oh, no . . .

Jake Hi!

Sally (*coolly*) Hallo. What do you want?

Jake I was just wondering if Madame – er . . . Miss –

Sally She's finishing her lunch.

Jake Ah. You haven't seen my dad, have you? Looking for him.

Sally Not since he chased out after your mother. (*to Gavin*) This is Jake.

Jake Hi.

Gavin Hallo, Jake. Gavin Ryng-Mayne. With a Y. How do you do?

Jake Hallo. (*slight pause*) Is that your car? The Porsche?

Gavin You got it.

Jake The yellow one.

Gavin That's the one.

Jake Cool. (*He stands there.*)

Sally What were we talking about? Wine, weren't we? So, how can you tell if they're any good?

Gavin Well, there are several ways. First, you look at the colour. Look, hold up the glass to the light and then tip it ever so slightly. That's it.

Sally (*doing this*) What am I looking for?

Gavin Well, you'll see that's a reddish brown which is a good colour for a fine wine. That means it's fully mature.

Wine can vary from purplish – which indicates a very young wine – to a sort of cherry red in a much lighter wine. Check it isn't cloudy which that certainly isn't – it's good and dark but not cloudy, that's important. Now. Next, you use your nose – hold the glass still . . . sniff the wine – deeply, that's it – now, swill it gently in the glass – good. Now, inhale again – Can you pick up all those varied flavours? Almost meaty, isn't it? What we call gamey . . .

Sally Yes, yes . . . musky . . . animal . . .

Jake Do you ever get around to drinking it, then?

Gavin Whooaa! Whooaa! Not so fast. Don't be so impatient. Make it last. Now the ultimate test. You need to taste it. Take a tiny sip – very, very little – and hold it in your mouth – right? – now, suck in a little air so that it circulates round your entire buccal cavity. Good. You should feel even more aromas at the back of your nose now, as the wine warms up – close your eyes, just enjoy the sensation on your tongue, let it invade all the passages. Yes? Now, savour it . . . enjoy it . . . allow it to linger . . .

Sally (*her mouth full of wine*) Yes . . . yes . . .

Gavin Now, if you must, you can swallow.

Sally (*doing so*) Wow.

A silence.

Jake Well, I'll . . . I'll be out here. When she's ready. (*He goes.*)

Gavin Friend of yours?

Sally Well. Vaguely.

Gavin Boy-friend?

Sally God, no. Well, I think he'd like to think he is. But he isn't. Not at all.

Gavin You don't have boy-friends?

Sally Sometimes. But not just at present. I'm too busy with other things.

Gavin Such as?

Sally Well, without wanting to sound selfish, my own future, really.

Gavin Anything particular in mind?

Sally I don't know yet. I might possibly go into politics. I'm quite keen to do that at present.

Gavin Politics? Oh, do beware!

Sally That's one possibility. National politics, of course, not local. I'm not interested in stray dogs or one-way traffic schemes. But then I write. So I might do that.

Gavin You write? How fascinating. Novels?

Sally Poetry, mainly. I find that more satisfying. I've written quite a lot, actually. Some of it's pretty good.

Gavin (*deadpan*) I'm sure it is. Who's your publisher?

Sally Oh, I haven't bothered to publish. Not yet. You need to have enough for a full anthology before you publish.

Gavin Oh, how very sensible. I remember Ted Hughes saying to me very much the same thing . . .

Sally (*oblivious*) Then I design a bit, as well. So there's always that, of course.

Gavin Good gracious . . .

Sally Hard to choose at the moment.

Gavin Spoilt for choice.

Sally (*in full spate*) Just a bit. And then I want to read a lot more. And – learn about things. All sorts of things. That my limited, curriculum-led education hasn't prepared me for. Wine. Life. Life outside this place. I want to travel. I want to go abroad. I want to see things and meet lots of people. So I'm not really too interested in starting relationships with men whose lives seem to begin and end here. Does that sound callous?

Gavin No. It sounds perfectly normal.

Sally Have you travelled a lot?

Gavin Quite a bit.

Sally To research your books, was it?

Gavin Sometimes.

Sally I'm afraid I haven't read any of them. Sorry.

Gavin Ah, well. Never mind. Fortunately a lot of people have.

Sally I'm afraid I'm not really into reading thrillers.

Gavin Good, because I'm not into writing thrillers, either . . .

Sally Oh. I thought they were –

Gavin I regard them simply as novels. But I agree, I think that's how I've been categorised. It's an appalling habit these days, isn't it, wanting to put everything into neat pigeon-holes. It's what I call the Internet Culture. Everything has to be cross-referenced for easy access. Instantly down-loadable knowledge. The thriller writers' website. The best hundred comic writers' website. Britain's tallest female dramatists' website . . .

Sally The world's most distinguished totally bald composers' . . .

Gavin (*smiling*) Right.

Sally smiles at him. Fran enters from the front door.

Fran 'Llo. Back again.

Sally Hallo.

Gavin Hallo, there.

Fran You all finished your lunch, have you?

Sally I think Lucille's still in the dining room.

Fran Nearly time for the opening, isn't it?

Trish hurries on from the hall, dressed and ready.

Trish It certainly is. Come on, we're going to be dreadfully late.

Fran I'd better fetch her then, hadn't I? In here, you say?

Trish (*at the French windows*) We might just miss the rain. It's going to bucket down in a minute.

Fran opens the dining room doors. A burst of merriment from Teddy and Lucille as she does so. They are doing silly French and English noises to each other, which in their current condition, they both find hilarious.

Teddy (*in French gibberish*) Long-dong-dong-yong – yeeuurr-yeurr-yeuurr . . .

Lucille (*in English gibberish*) Yarrk-yaarrk-yarrah-ho-ho-ho-harr . . .

* **Fran** Voyons, Lucille, le moment est venu d'ouvrir la fête et de partir d'ici.

---

* Come on, Lucille, it's time to open the fête and get you away from here.

* **Lucille** Oh, vous! Quel rabat joie. Chaque fois que je m'amuse vous êtes toujours là pour tout gâcher . . .

Fran Mon Dieu, vous n'avez pas bu, dites-moi? Has she been drinking?

Teddy She's been initiated into the joys of single malt . . .

Fran Vous savez bien que vous ne devriez pas boire. Vous m'avez promis de ne pas boire.

Trish She had the odd glass of wine at lunch and then –

> *Lucille and Teddy remain in the dining room. They are both unnaturally merry rather than drunk.*

† **Lucille** Oh, mais qu'est-ce-que vous racontez? Un petit verre, pauvre pétasse. Qu'est-ce-que ça va changer? Si j'ai envie de boire, je boirai. Si je vous écoutais, je ne m'amuserais jamais. Je resterais dans mon coin, muette comme une bonne soeur.

Fran (*over this*) Why did you let her drink, for God's sake?

Trish What do you mean, let her drink?

Fran She shouldn't be drinking.

Sally Why not?

---

* **Lucille** Oh, it's you! Trust you to break up a good party. Whenever I'm enjoying myself you always manage to ruin it . . .

Fran My God, you haven't been drinking, have you? Has she been drinking?

Teddy She's been initiated into the joys of single malt . . .

Fran You know you shouldn't be drinking. You promised me you wouldn't drink.

† Oh, what are you going on about? One little drink, you miserable bitch. What difference is that going to make? If I want a drink I'll have a drink. If you had your way, I'd never get any fun at all. Just sit in silence like a nun.

Fran Because – because she has a problem with it. You should never have let her near a bloody drink . . .

Trish Well, we didn't know that.

Fran She's like Jekyll and Hyde. After three drinks, she's a liability . . .

Teddy (*from the dining room*) Lucille and I have worked out a perfect way of communication. We have entirely solved the entente koolibar . . . Naysapar?

Lucille (*likewise*) York-york-wobble-wobble-old bean . . .

Teddy Nyooon-onson-ponson-lanson-deeverrr . . . See, perfect understanding?

Trish Well, if you'd told us, we would never have offered her a drink in the first place . . . (*to Sally*) Let this be a lesson to you. (*to Fran*) Why didn't you warn us?

Fran Because I was sent off to the pub for lunch on my own, wasn't I?

Teddy See what I mean? She understands me perfectly. Yakkerdoo-bien – arrrbeurrrr . . .

Trish Yes . . . But I thought . . . That's what you'd prefer to do. As her chauffeur. The chauffeurs usually prefer to do that.

Lucille Hugh-hugh-hugh-bla-bla-bla . . .

Fran I'm not her chauffeur. I work in her agent's office.

Trish Oh, I see. I do beg your pardon. You should have said. I assumed you were the chauffeur.

Teddy She's been getting a bit uppity about inferior French market produce. I was forced to remind her of Agincourt . . .

Lucille (*attacking him*) Pah, Agincourt . . . Agincourt . . .

Teddy (*retreating round the table*) Oui, Agincourt . . .

Fran (*pursuing him*) Not everyone who drives a car's a chauffeur, you know.

Teddy Enri le sank. Waterloo!

Trish No, I'm sorry I . . .

Lucille Oui, Waterloo. Napoleon.

Fran Not everyone who opens doors is a doorman . . .

Teddy (*counter-attacking Lucille*) Wellington!

Trish No, there's been some dreadful confusion, I've said I'm terribly sorry. Did you have a pleasant lunch, anyway?

Lucille (*retreating into the sitting room*) Napoleon!

Fran Yes I did, thank you. Very nice rare roast beef . . .

Teddy (*pursuing her*) Wellington!

Sally Lucky you.

Lucille Napoleon! (*She loses her footing and sits on the floor.*)

Trish Oh dear, this is terrible. She doesn't even look as if she can stand up . . .

Teddy She'll be fine, she's fine . . .

Barry, a lively man in his thirties and undoubtedly the organising energy behind the garden fête, appears at the French windows.

Barry (*to Gavin*) Good afternoon. Good afternoon, Sally. Good afternoon, Patricia. I –

* **Lucille** Oh, chouette! Encore ce drôle de petit bonhomme! Celui qu'on a recontré tout à l'heure!

---

* Oh, good! Here's that funny little man again! The one we met earlier!

Fran I don't think she's up to it. I think you'd better find someone else.

* **Lucille** L'idiot du village! I – declare this – fête – open . . .

    Fran takes a grip on Lucille.

(*resenting this*) Ne me touchez pas! Je peux marcher, je peux marcher très bien, toute seule, merci . . .

Fran Pourquoi est-ce-que vous faites ça? Regardez de quoi vous avez l'air, vous pouvez à peine tenir debout.

Lucille Je tiens très bien debout, ne vous inquiétez pas. Vous roulerez sous la table bien avant moi . . .

Fran Ça, j'en suis sûre . . .

Barry Is there a problem?

Trish No, no problem, Barry, she's just . . .

Sally Shouldn't she go and lie down?

Lucille Teddy . . .!

Teddy Wah-wu-war-war-war-mon-brave . . .

Trish I'm sure she'll be fine, once she's in the fresh air. All she has to do is open the thing . . . she doesn't have to hang around . . .

† **Lucille** Teddy. Teddy, prenez mon bras . . .

---

* **Lucille** The village idiot! I – declare this – fête – open . . .

    Fran takes a grip on Lucille.

(*resenting this*) Don't manhandle me! I can walk, I can walk perfectly well on my own, thank you . . .

Fran Why do you do it? Look at you, you can hardly stand up.

Lucille I can stand up, don't worry. I can drink you under the table . . .

Fran I'm sure of that . . .

† Teddy. Teddy, hold my arm . . .

Fran (*to Teddy*) Can you take her arm? She wants you to take her arm.

Teddy (*doing so*) Most certainly. Yuwoo-deezurs . . .

* **Lucille** Ah, Teddy, mon ami Teddy! York-york-york.

Trish Are we going to miss the rain, Barry?

Barry We might. We might be lucky, Patricia, if we hurry . . .

> *Barry, Lucille, Fran and Teddy go out on to the terrace. As they are going, Fran's mobile rings. Under the next, she locates it and answers it in the dining room. Gavin and Sally seem in no hurry to follow them. Trish also lingers.*

Trish Come on, Sally, we need you down there, too.

Sally I think I might come down a bit later . . .

Trish No, now. Come on.

Sally I don't happen to –

Trish (*firmly, sotto*) Sally, please. Do as I ask. Please.

Sally For God's sake! (*Sally stamps off through the door to the hall, embarrassed in front of Gavin. Angrily, over her shoulder as she goes*) See what I mean?

> *A rumble of thunder.*

Trish Now where are you going?

Sally (*off*) To get a coat, of course.

Trish (*to Gavin*) Oh, dear. It's so easy to offend them, isn't it? At that age?

Fran (*during this, on the terrace*) . . . Yes . . . yes . . . yes . . . no, that's the point, she's back on it . . . yes . . .

---

* Ah, Teddy! My friend, Teddy! York-york-york.

quite a bit by the look of it . . . Well, I wasn't invited to lunch, was I? Otherwise, I . . . Yes, I will. She's just going to open it, yes . . . No, that's alright, I don't think there are . . . Not even a photographer. I don't think they have newspapers in this part of the world . . . Yes, I will. Soon as I've delivered her. Yes . . . yes . . . OK. (*She disconnects.*) Shit. (*to Trish*) Where'd they all go?

Trish Down on the lower meadow there. Down the steps.

Gavin Where are you delivering her? Hollyhurst?

Fran Who told you that?

Gavin Just two and two put together, really.

Fran Well, do me a favour and don't make that four, alright? We don't want it public. No press here today, are there? I didn't see any.

Trish Just our local paper. I think Jake is trying to get a word with her, if he –

Fran Shit. (*She moves rapidly through the French windows and runs off.*)

More thunder.

Trish What on earth is Hollyhurst?

Gavin It's a very smart, very expensive, very exclusive clinic. Used by the rich and famous to help quell their foolish habits . . .

Trish Oh, it's a clinic! I've never heard of it, I'm afraid.

Gavin Just as it should be.

Trish Well. You have children these days, you hold your breath and pray. Do you have children?

Gavin No.

Trish You're married, though?

Gavin No.

Trish Oh. I somehow thought you were. Don't know where I got that idea. You were married though, weren't you?

Gavin No.

Trish Oh.

A pause.

(*laughing*) Well, now we know all about you then, don't we?

Gavin And I'm not gay either. Before you ask . . .

Trish No, no, I didn't. Gosh, no. I never thought you were. Heavens, no. Not that I'm – I mean, fine. If you were. But. Super.

Gavin I was, mind you.

Trish Gay?

Gavin Yes. At one stage of my life. But I gave it up.

Trish Really. Why was that?

Gavin I don't know. I think it all just got rather – tedious.

Trish Ah.

Gavin There was an awful lot of hard work to it, you know.

Trish Yes. I can imagine.

Gavin Emotional hard work.

Trish Yes, yes . . .

Gavin Men tend to take it out on each other, rather.

Trish Yes, I can see they might, yes.

Gavin So I – changed shirts, as they say.

Trish Yes, that's very interesting. And are you – happier now?

Gavin Oh, yes.

Trish Good. Good. (*Slight pause.*) That's the main thing, isn't it? I don't know why she's taking so long to get a coat, for heaven's sake. Perhaps she's changing her shirt. (*She laughs. A slight pause.*) She's seventeen, that's all I'm saying. Just seventeen.

> *Pause.*

Why don't I trust you for some reason? I ought to be able to trust you, I'm sure. But it's rather like finding a fox in one's chicken run.

> *She laughs. Gavin smiles.*
> *Another silence.*

I think you must have gathered that things between Teddy and me have reached a rather peculiar state, just at present.

Gavin Yes, I had noticed.

Trish It's very hard, you see, for someone like me. I'm originally from a navy background, I don't know if you knew?

Gavin I did read that somewhere.

Trish My father was pretty high ranking. He was a rear admiral, actually.

Gavin Yes, I did know that.

Trish And my mother was really of the old school – fiercely loyal. I mean *fiercely* loyal. It was my father first and foremost, all the time, absolutely, without question. And we were all girls, four of us – he desperately wanted a boy but he never got one, poor man – and the four of us, we were unquestionably background. You put your man first. Have a career, by all means, if you really have to – but when the chips were down, the man came first.

Gavin But you did have a career?

Trish Oh, yes I – messed around – designing bits and pieces . . .

Gavin Come on, it was very successful design practice . . .

Trish Yes, it was . . .

Gavin In which you were offered a partnership, weren't you?

Trish Yes, but they were desperately short of people. They were taking on anyone, really, at that time . . .

Gavin A partnership before you were thirty? I don't know much about these things but I'd have thought that was fairly impressive.

Trish Well, it wasn't bad, but – You know an awful lot about me. How do you know all this?

Gavin Oh. I'm always listening out. I hear things.

Trish Anyway. I got the job to do up this place. Of course, I met Teddy. His father was still alive then. And one thing led to – another.

Gavin And then you gave it all up?

Trish Well, I was expecting Sally and – we're a long way from London. You get a bit out of the swing, you know. But lately, things have been a bit tricky. You mustn't think they're always like this.

Gavin No.

Trish Actually, they're usually worse. (*She laughs.*) Oh God, I'm sorry I shouldn't say that. You see, I saw my mother standing by this man – by my father – making sure we all stood by him – and it was only about ten years after he died that I realised, bloody rear-admiral or not, he wasn't worth tuppence. Not compared to my mother. He was a humourless, insensitive, self-righteous, self-opinionated, callous, bully. And when he died, shortly afterwards, she died. Because he'd allowed her no reason of her own to carry on living. That's what it amounted to. Everybody said she died of grief which was absolute bollocks. She died because her life was totally pointless. All the same, it's very difficult to break the tradition, you see. My sisters all find it the same with their marriages – well, Joan isn't married, but she might as well be, she's shacked up with this fearful creature – but we're all, at heart, little rear-admiral's wives . . . It's very hard to break out of that. My way of coping is to blot things out completely. I've started editing my life. Like a stencil, you know. You hold it over the paper and you just allow the bit you want to bleed through. It works reasonably well. Most people are coming to the conclusion that I'm going completely batty – but since I'm obviously harmless, they're happy to humour me.

Gavin It can't go on, though, can it?

Trish No. It can't, of course it can't.

Gavin I take it a rapprochement is not on the cards?

Trish Oh, golly, no. Long past that, I'm afraid. I think I should get out, really, shouldn't I? But I don't know. Where do I go? What do I do? Nice comfy life here, in many ways. Plenty of money. Daughter doing her A-levels. All sorts of things to consider. And then I feel – no! In any case, that's not fitting conduct for an admiral's daughter. In my family, the women go down with the ship.

Gavin Be careful. I was hearing earlier about the women in the Platt family . . .

Trish Yes, dreadful, isn't it? Do you think we're all cursed? I sometimes sit here in the evening and there's old Cat Platt looking at me saying, you're next! (*Pause.*) I suppose telling you all this isn't doing Teddy's chances a lot of good, is it? I mean, I don't really know why you're here but it's obviously something quite important. I don't want to be told, don't worry. It's just, whatever there is between us, I wouldn't want to spoil his chances – despite everything he's done.

Gavin Well, spouses aren't supposed to be part of the equation these days. They still are, of course, very often. But we're not supposed to notice any more if the Foreign Secretary's partner is chewing up the family rug.

Sally returns. She has changed completely into a new outfit. She has also applied additional, quite subtle make-up. The others stop and look at her.

Sally Hallo. (*looking at them*) What's the matter?

Trish What?

Sally Why are you staring?

Trish You went to get a coat. You've changed completely.

Sally I thought I'd dress up for this fête, that's all. What's wrong?

Trish I don't know why you've got all that lot on to stand in a drizzle selling tombola tickets . . .

Sally Alright, I'll go and change again . . .

Trish No, no . . .

Sally If you think I look ridiculous . . .

Trish I didn't say you looked ridiculous. For heaven's sake, Sally, what's got into you? All I said was – you look a bit – overdressed. For a garden fête. That's all.

Pause.

Sally So you do want me to change?

Trish (*snapping*) No, I don't want you to change. I don't care if you come dressed as a scuba diver. I'm going on down there. Are you coming?

Sally I'm coming.

Trish hesitates.

Trish You are coming? Promise me.

Sally *Yes.*

Gavin We'll be down. Promise.

Trish looks at them both anxiously. She can think of no further reason to stay.

Trish (*anxiously*) Right.

Trish goes. A big clap of thunder.

Gavin That doesn't sound so good . . .

Sally What were you both talking about just then? Me, I bet.

Gavin No.

Sally Bet you were.

Gavin Actually, we were talking about your mother. Chiefly.

Sally Oh. I see. I go upstairs for five minutes and you start chatting her up as well.

Gavin Is that what I've been doing? Chatting you up?

Sally Yes. Weren't you?

Before he can reply, the terrace becomes filled with people. Trish, Barry, Izzie, Jake and a group of children. Also Lindy, Barry's wife, dogsbody and occasional scapegoat.

Trish Well, that was short and sweet. It's absolutely bucketing down. Come in everyone. Come along in . . .

Lindy I think the children had better stay out here, Patricia, under the awning. They're all drenched. They'd wreck your lovely room.

Trish OK. Just as you like. I'll organise some tea and juice and things – Izzie, could you mastermind that?

Jake walks into the room but stops when he sees Gavin and Sally.

Jake (*coolly*) Hallo.

Sally (*likewise*) Hallo.

Gavin Hi, Jake.

In a second, Jake wanders back on to the terrace, where Barry seems to be entertaining the children with a game of I-spy, then a sing-song.

Izzie (*looking around, suspiciously*) Where is she? Where's she got to?

Trish Who's that?

Izzie Pearl. The Jezebel's still out there with him. I warned 'em, I warned 'em! (*Izzie goes out through the French windows, and off into the garden, pushing through the others.*)

Trish Izzie, you'll get soak – Oh, for goodness sake . . .

Pearl comes in from the hall with her camera.

Pearl What's happened? Rained off, is it?

Trish Oh, Pearl, there you are. What are you doing?

Pearl Just fetching my camera . . . Not much use now, is it?

Trish Izzie just went out looking for you. She seemed rather agitated.

Pearl (*in sudden alarm*) Oh, my God. He better be alright. If she lays a finger on him, I'll murder her . . . (*Pearl rushes out on to the terrace and follows Izzie off.*)

Trish Lord . . .

Gavin A crisis?

Trish Heaven knows.

Sally There's always a crisis with those three . . .

Lindy comes into the room cautiously.

Lindy Can I be of any help at all, Patricia? If you're making tea?

Trish Thank you, Lindy. Since the entire domestic staff seem to be having some sort of drama in the rain, that would be much appreciated.

Lindy Always happy to do something . . . (*She sniffs.*)

Trish You OK?

Lindy Yes. Just one of those days, you know. You get them, don't you? When you just can't seem to do anything right?

Trish Oh, dear. Yes, I get those frequently. Come and tell me about it.

Fran (*through the doorway, to Trish*) Any idea where your husband and Lucille went?

Trish (*sweetly*) None at all, I'm afraid. Haven't seen him all day.

Fran (*muttering*) Oh, bloody film stars . . .

Lindy and Trish go off to the kitchen. Fran goes off into the garden, braving the rain.

Barry (*from the terrace*) I think there'll be a rainbow in a minute, children . . .

Sally Do you mind if I close these doors? It's a bit drafty.

Sally does so. The next is played quite lightly. Two people playing games on the edge of a cliff. Softly, led by Barry, the children sing 'Jesus bids us shine' under the next.

So you deny you were chatting me up, do you?

Gavin I didn't deny it.

Sally (*self-consciously casual*) So what are you going to do about it?

Gavin What do you suggest I do?

Sally I don't know. We could go upstairs, I suppose.

Gavin (*smiling*) Risky. Your mother only downstairs. What would she think?

Sally She wouldn't care.

Gavin Don't you believe it.

Sally We could go out somewhere. For a drive. In your lovely smart car.

Gavin You'd like that?

Sally Love it. I love fast cars. And perhaps – we could stop somewhere . . .

Gavin . . . for dinner . . .

Sally . . . at some smart hotel . . .

Gavin . . . five star . . .

Sally . . . and we could sniff some more wine together . . .

Gavin . . . just a little . . .

Sally . . . and then – who knows?

Gavin We could go upstairs to our huge double room . . .

Sally . . . four poster bed . . .

Gavin . . . at least . . .

Sally . . . and then we'd . . .

Gavin . . . undress each other . . .

Sally . . . if you like . . .

Gavin . . . and we'd indulge in sheer shameless hedonistic pleasure . . .

Sally Sheer shameless hedonistic pleasure, I like that. And what would that be for you? What's your idea of shameless hedonistic pleasure? What would I have to do to please you?

Gavin Me? Oh, I've very simple tastes.

Sally What? Tell me. Come on. You're not going to shock me, you know. Go on. You're not, you know.

Gavin Alright. Well, we'd go into the bathroom where I'd run you a deep, piping hot bath, scented with an exotic bath essence, courtesy of Crabtree and Evelyn.

Sally Sounds nice.

Gavin And you'd lie in that bath until you were pink and glowing all over. Then you'd get out and I'd ever so gently pat you dry with a big soft, pure white towel. With me so far?

Sally Sure.

Gavin And then you'd get dressed again.

Sally I would?

Gavin Only this time in your school uniform. The one you were wearing today when I first saw you . . .

Sally (*startled*) My school uniform . . .?

Gavin (*leaning in close to her*) And then you'd get under the shower and turn it to the coldest setting until you were soaked to the skin and shivering . . .

Sally (*somewhat bemused*) What?

Gavin And then I'd hand you the Gideon Bible and you'd go outside, still wet through, into the hall, closing the door behind you; you'd count to ten and then ring the bell. And when I opened it, you'd say, good evening sir, I bring good news of mankind's salvation, are you by any chance a sinner? And I'd say, yes my dear, I fear that I am, but I am certain I can be saved. Please come inside and allow me to offer you dry clothes for I see you are drenched through. And I'd lead you into the bedroom, remove your nasty wet uniform, put you over my knee and spank you soundly with your own bible for being a bumptious, flirtatious, precocious, conceited, smug little prick-teaser.

Sally (*completely shattered*) Oh. (*suddenly feeling a bit sick*) I – Oh.

> *Sally rushes off through the hall door. She nearly collides with first Trish, then Lindy. Trish is carrying a plate of biscuits, Lindy has a tray of orange juice and mugs of tea.*
>
> *Simultaneously, Jake who has been watching the exchange between Sally and Gavin through the terrace*

windows, comes through the French doors, closing them behind him, and glares at Gavin. Gavin shrugs and smiles.

Trish (*as Sally goes off*) Sally . . .?

Lindy Whoops!

Trish (*to Gavin*) What's going on? Why did she rush off like that?

Gavin I've no idea. At that age . . . you know. Over-excitement perhaps?

Jake crosses swiftly and goes off into the hall after Sally. The rain has now stopped and people are leaving the shelter of the terrace.

Trish Jake? What's got into everyone suddenly?

Gavin (*seeing the biscuits*) Oh, may I? These look delicious.

Trish They're meant for the kids. (*going back into the hall, calling*) Sally . . . Sally . . .

Trish goes out. Lindy meanwhile has reached the French windows with the tray, in time to see everyone leaving. She calls to Barry, the last to leave.

Lindy Would you open the door, please, dear?

Barry (*without opening the doors*) What's that?

Lindy Brought the tea and the orange juice for you all . . .

Barry Too late now.

Lindy Oh.

Barry Need you back there. Come on. Hurry up! Hurry up!

Barry hurries off to the garden.

Lindy (*sadly*) Take them back, I suppose. (*She starts on her way back.*)

Gavin (*as she passes, taking an orange juice*) Thank you.

Lindy That's for the children.

Gavin (*taking a sip*) Delicious.

> *Lindy goes out by the hall door.*
> *Gavin drains his glass.*
> *He moves to the French windows as if to go out.*
> *Jake returns from the hall.*

Jake (*in quiet anger*) Excuse me.

Gavin (*pleasantly*) Jake?

Jake I'd like a – like a – like a word, please.

Gavin It is Jake, isn't it? I used to have a dog called Jake, you know.

Jake What did you say to Sally just now? What did you say to her?

Gavin Cocker spaniel. Had to have him put down. Broke my heart.

Jake Just now. When you were in here together. I was watching through the – through the window. She was extremely upset. She's just run out of the front door.

Gavin Oh dear, has she? Well, I've no idea what can have upset her.

> *Lindy re-enters from the hall.*

Jake You know bloody well . . .

> *He stops as he sees Lindy. Lindy, realising she has interrupted something rather tense, tip-toes past them self-consciously.*

Lindy (*quietly*) Excuse me.

> *Lindy goes out through the French windows. Gavin makes as if to follow. Jake crosses to him and makes to block Gavin's path.*

Jake Just a minute! I want to know what – know what – know what – upset Sally.

Gavin Perhaps you should ask her, old boy.

Jake I just tried. She was so up – so up – so upset she wouldn't even speak to me.

Gavin I'm afraid that's your problem . . .

Jake Oh, no . . .

Gavin . . . if she won't even speak to you . . .

Jake This is our problem. Yours and – yours and – yours and mine.

Gavin Oh, come now. Stop behaving like a schoolboy.

> *Jake stands confronting him.*

Out of my way.

Jake Not till we've talked about it. I want to know what happened.

Gavin Out of my way, please. (*He tries to move past Jake but his path is blocked.*) Come along, now. Don't let it get silly . . . (*He tries to get past again.*) I'll only ask you once more, Jake.

> *He tries to move past rather more forcefully. Jake pushes him back.*

Now, you're starting to annoy me . . .

Jake Good.

Gavin Get out of my way, please.

He tries again. Jake repeats the push. Gavin moves with great speed, flooring Jake with a sharp punch in the face. Jake sits heavily on the floor, startled rather than badly hurt.

Now I did ask you nicely. I wouldn't get up again, if I were you. Next time I really will hurt you, old boy.

Gavin strolls out and goes off into the garden. Jake sits on the floor examining his face gingerly.

Jake Ow.

Trish returns.

Trish Well, I don't know what's got into her, she's nowhere in the house, she's not in her room – Jake, what on earth are you doing now?

Jake (*lamely*) I – er – I fell – I fell – I fell – slipped –

Trish Oh, dear. You alright?

Jake Yes, I – Yes. (*indicating he should leave*) I'll –

Trish Sit down for a minute, Jake.

Jake I really ought to – ought to –

Trish Please. Just for a minute.

Jake does so. Trish follows suit.

What really happened?

Jake He – he ups – upset Sally.

Trish Gavin? Yes, I saw he had.

Jake I – tackled him about it. That's all.

Trish Well, that was brave of you, Jake, but actually extremely foolhardy. People like Gavin are quite dangerous. I was trying to think what it was about him, earlier. I couldn't put my finger on it at first. What it is about him, of course, is that he's completely – devoid of real feeling. No genuine emotion, not even sexual. He's not a fox, I was wrong. He's more a lizard. So nothing really can reach him. Which is what makes him dangerous because people like that can so easily manipulate the rest of us, who do feel, who do care. You see?

Jake What was he doing with Sally, then? If he wasn't –

Trish He was playing a nasty little game with her that's all, Jake. Nothing to worry about. Hopefully all that's been hurt is her pride. You'll need to be specially nice to her for a day or two, that's all.

Jake If I can get close enough.

Trish Oh, don't worry . . .

Jake She seems to want to push me away half the time. Just ignores me. Then other times . . .

Trish Oh, well, that's all part of it, isn't it? This ridiculous dance we all do – if we're not born Gavin Ryng-Maynes, that is. You know, the other evening I was out there in the garden watching the village children with Joanna – with your mother – rehearsing their Maypole dance. There they were, all clinging to their coloured ribbons as if their lives depended on it. Well, judging from Joanna's tone of voice they probably did. And I thought, that's how it is for all of us, really. When we're young we're each given a ribbon – we're desperate for a ribbon – any ribbon – to cling on to – and once we have our ribbon we're taught the dance. And from then on, for the rest of our lives, we obediently move round and round our Maypole, observing respective little set patterns, weaving in and out, keeping our distances, careful never to step on each other's toes . . . Clinging on to our ribbon, terrified of deviating in case we get hurt or lost or rejected. But the older we get, despite all our efforts, the more we get entangled with other people. Yet never for a minute do most of us ever dream of doing the obvious and just letting go. We're terrified. The hardest thing believe me sometimes, Jake, is never to take hold of a ribbon, never to join the bloody dance in the first place; but actually stand still and say to someone, I love you. And mean it. You'd think it would be so simple, wouldn't you?

Jake Do you think she loves me?

Trish I'd have thought so, wouldn't you? You don't go to all that trouble for someone you don't like. You don't bother to dance at all.

Jake If only she'd say . . .

Trish Well, to be fair. Have you ever said it to her?

Jake What, I love you?

Trish Have you? In so many words?

Jake Well, I've – I think I've – shown it – in the way I've –

Trish Takes two, Jake. Go on. Give it a try sometime. What's the worst she can she say? Too bad, buster.

Jake That's what I'm afraid of . . .

Trish (*getting up, smiling*) Garn! Plenty more girls, aren't there? Gorgeous bloke like you . . .

She turns to go back through the hall door. Pearl is suddenly standing there, breathing hard and somewhat déshabillé in her fortune-teller's outfit.

Pearl . . .

Pearl Sssshhh! She's after me.

Trish Oh, God. Now what? Who's after you, Pearl?

94

Pearl Her. She said she'd get us and now she's out to get me . . .

Trish Pearl, for goodness sake. Who is out to get you? If you'd only –

Izzie appears in the front windows. She is holding a very large carving knife. Pearl screams.

(*seeing her*) – oh, dear God!

Pearl (*with a scream*) No!!! (*She rushes into the dining room and closes the doors behind her.*)

Trish Pearl! Izzie, what are you doing?

Izzie I just want to talk to her, that's all, Patricia. I just want to talk –

Trish Well, why have you got the knife, Izzie? Do you need the knife to talk to Pearl?

Izzie I cut 'em. I cut 'em, you see.

Trish You cut them. Who did you cut?

Izzie I cut the guys. I cut right through the guys.

Jake Which guys?

Trish Which guys, Izzie? Who are we talking about?

Izzie I didn't mean to cut their guys. I thought it were them two. That's why I cut the guys. I thought it were them there.

Trish Izzie, just give me the knife, please.

Trish moves forward and holds out her hand. Izzie draws back and waves the blade threateningly.

Izzie No!

Trish Izzie! (*to Jake*) Warn. We need Warn, Jake. Can you fetch him here? He may be able to sort this out . . .

Jake Will you be alright?

Trish Just find Warn . . .

Jake Unless she's killed him . . .

Trish Oh, God, I hadn't thought of that. Izzie, you haven't killed Warn, have you? You haven't hurt Warn? God, we'd never find another gardener.

Izzie I didn't mean to hurt no one. I just cut the guys.

Jake Who's she talking about?

Trish I don't know who she's talking about. Off you go. Quick as you can . . .

Jake dashes out of the French windows.

Izzie would you please put down the knife. Then we can talk properly. I'm going to bring Pearl out here, then we can talk about it sensibly. There's no need for knives. There's never any need for knives. (*knocking on the dining room doors*) Pearl . . . Pearl . . .

Pearl (*muffled, from within*) Don't let her in here . . .

Trish Pearl, stand away from this door. I'm coming in.

Pearl She's not coming in here, she's not –

Trish It's only me. I'm coming in.

Trish opens the door. A plate is hurled and smashes against the dining room wall – some distance from Trish but still close enough to cause her to close the door sharply.

Dear God! It's getting like a war zone.

Muffled muttering from Pearl.

Pearl, please don't do that. That is not helping.

More muffled muttering from Pearl.

If you do that again, I shall dock it from your money. Now, I'm coming in, Pearl . . .

Trish opens the door a fraction. Another plate smashes.

Oh, Lord. Izzie, can't you do something?

Further muffled muttering from Pearl.

Pearl, if you want to throw plates, can you throw the service with the gold rim. You've already broken so many of those it doesn't matter. But not the Crown Derby, please.

Pearl mutters some more.

(*in despair*) I don't know what to do. I really don't know what to do. I think I'm just going to go to bed.

Pearl continues to mutter.

(*angrily*) Pearl! I am fast losing patience. Pearl! (*She thumps on the door.*)

Another smash.

That was. That was the Crown Derby. I recognised it.

Warn, the gardener appears at the French windows with Jake following. He is probably in his late fifties or early sixties but he is not a man whose age it is easy to assess.

Trish Oh, Warn, thank heavens . . .

Jake He was already on his way . . .

Trish Warn, can you possibly sort this out?

Warn (*walking briskly into the room, to Izzie*) Give that to me. Cut yourself.

Izzie hands the knife over without a murmur.

(*indicating the dining room*) In there?

Trish Yes.

Warn (*shouting through the door*) Pearl! (*Silence.*) Pearl! (*Silence.*) Pearl!

Pearl (*at last, from within*) Who is it?

Warn Who d'you think? It's Warn.

Silence from within.

Pearl! D'you hear me? Come on out, now. It's Warn.

Silence.

Come on then, girl! Come on. It's . . . It's . . .

He looks at Izzie. She nods encouragingly.

(*with great difficulty*) It's . . . dad. It's your dad.

Izzie (*softly*) Oh, Warn!

A slight pause. The dining room door slowly opens. Pearl appears.

Pearl (*tentatively*) Dad? Dad?

Warn Come on. Go home now.

He puts an arm round her. They move towards the French windows. Izzie rushes to join them.

Izzie (*letting it all spill out*) He never would before, you see, he never would. I said to him when I moved in, I said, now it's got to be different, you see, with me being her mum, that would make you like her dad. It don't matter what he was before, he has to be her dad, now her mum's moved in, don't he? 'Sides, Pearl needed a dad more than anything, 'cause she didn't have one not originally, 'cause he pissed off, the bugger, and I never saw him not after that one night and a girl needs a dad, she needs someone to clip her round the ear, but Warn never would, you see, 'cause he thought it were wrong but it can't never be wrong for a girl to have a dad, can

98

it? But now it's going to be alright, you see? It's all worked out now and we're all proper and circumcised at last.

Izzie, Pearl and Warn go out into the garden.

Trish I can't pretend to understand what that was about.

Jake shrugs.

As I was saying. Love is essentially a very simple business. But in the hands of human beings it often becomes monstrously complicated.

Teddy and Lucille arrive at the French windows. They are both extremely bedraggled and wet and muddy. She has no shoes. He has no shoes, socks or trousers. Trish and Jake stare at them.

Teddy 'Fraid we both got caught in the rain . . .

Trish goes out through the hall door slamming it behind her.

Still not bloody talking to me, is she?

The lights fade to:
  Blackout.

SCENE TWO

Saturday, August 14th, 5.00 p.m.
  Gavin is standing by the windows. Teddy comes in from the hall. He has now changed and smartened up a bit.

Teddy Ah, here you are . . .

Gavin Teddy, I'm just off – I've said good-bye to Trish – I just wanted to thank you for a fabulous day. Thoroughly enjoyable.

Teddy Yes? Oh, good . . .

Gavin I do envy you all this. I mean, stuck in the smoke there, you really forget what real life's about, don't you? I do hope you'll ask me down again some time . . .

Teddy Yes, of course. Always welcome.

Gavin Will you say good-bye to Sally for me? I'm afraid I've managed to miss her . . .

Teddy Yes, I'll say –

Gavin Lovely girl, Teddy. You must be very proud. Bright as a button, isn't she? Good brain on her.

Teddy Yes, well, I don't know where that comes from, I'm sure . . . (*He laughs.*)

Gavin No, seriously, Teddy. Credit to you both. It says a great deal for the future of this country if we've got young people like that in the pipeline.

Teddy Yes. Yes. True.

A brief silence.

Gavin (*making to leave*) Well . . .

Teddy Er . . . I'm taking it the – offer of – of political candidacy is not currently still on the cards . . .

Gavin Well . . .

Teddy No, no, no. Just wanted to clear it up . . .

Gavin You know, Teddy, seeing you here – amongst all this – the social life, the family – the commitment you have to the local people – the irons in the fire – so many fish to fry – I just don't think you'd have time for it all, Teddy. With the best will in the world. I mean, these days an MP's job – nose to the grindstone, Teddy – and, let's face it, desperately single-track stuff . . .

Teddy Yes, yes, yes . . .

Gavin I mean, if I was to sum you up – which I shall be doing, incidentally, to the PM when I see him – I'd be tempted to describe you as a good old-fashioned renaissance man, Teddy . . .

Teddy Would you? Would you?

Gavin And, God bless you, I wish there were more of you. Bloody specialisation, be the death of us all . . .

Teddy That's always been my view . . .

Gavin So. Short answer. Don't expect the call but not to worry. I'll explain to the PM your reasons for turning it down and as you know, he's nothing if not reasonable. I know he'll be absolutely flat-batted, but I'm certain he'll understand. OK? Must dash. Don't see me off, please. I know you have masses to do. Take care, old boy, wonderful to see you. I'll be in touch very soon. 'Bye.

Teddy 'Bye.

Gavin (*as he goes*) Incidentally, terrific wine, too. (*He goes off into the garden.*)

Teddy Ah, well. Can't win 'em all, I suppose . . .

He is about to go into the dining room when Fran comes in from the hall.

Fran She's just about ready now. I'm going to fetch the car. I'll bring it round to the front, alright?

Teddy No, don't bother, I'll walk Lucille down – I'll walk down with her through the garden.

Fran Sure?

Teddy Say good-bye properly.

Fran Well, don't take any more detours, will you? I have to deliver her to that place and then get back to London tonight.

Teddy How long is she likely to be there, do you know?

Fran No idea. A week or so. Why?

Teddy I just thought I might visit her. Must get a bit dull in those places.

Fran Suit yourself. Do us a favour, just take her a bunch of flowers if you do.

Fran goes off into the garden.
    Teddy goes into the dining room. Trish comes in from the hall. She looks for Teddy, sees he is in the dining room and goes and sits in a chair in the sitting room and waits. Teddy comes out of the dining room. He has a large whisky. He sees Trish but, accustomed to her silence, chooses to ignore her. He sits in another chair and sips his whisky. Silence.

Trish (*quite suddenly*) Teddy . . .

Teddy (*whisky slopping all over him*) Oh, my God! Would you kindly not do that?

Trish Sorry. I have something to say to you, Teddy.

Teddy Oh well, super. Three weeks of total silence and suddenly we're going to get a speech, are we?

Trish Teddy . . .

Teddy Whoopee! I can't wait.

Trish Teddy . . .

Teddy Hang on a tick, I'll get the cassette recorder, just in case it's the last words you ever say to me. Like a permanent record, you know. Just for the family archives. These are the wife's last words. Thought you'd like to hear them.

Trish Teddy! These may well be my last words. To you. They might well.

Teddy (*a little startled*) What? You haven't – er . . . You haven't done anything stupid, have you?

Trish Like what?

Teddy I don't know. You haven't taken poison or something?

Trish No, of course I haven't. If I was going to poison anyone, it would be you.

Teddy (*laughs, then*) You haven't, have you?

Trish Teddy. The point is, I'm leaving. I've tried to avoid this. It's against everything I stand for. Desertion. Walking off a sink – But I can feel it, Teddy. The curse of the Platt women. It's there, breathing heavily. Just behind me. I have to go. I'm sorry. I've discussed this with Sally, don't worry, and she fully understands. She said if it wasn't for her A-levels she'd come with me. So you won't be entirely abandoned. You'll also have Izzie and you'll have Pearl, God help you . . . You'll have masses of people to look after you, so don't worry . . .

Teddy Just no wife . . .?

Trish You haven't had a wife for ages, Teddy, what are you talking about? More important, with me out of the way, you can get a clear run of the field. You can have the entire village. Droit de seigneur. Whatever you fancy, be my guest.

Teddy I see.

Trish That's all I wanted to say. So – cheerio, really. I wish I could say it's been fun but these last few years have been utter hell. I don't know how I've put up with it for as long as I have, actually. (*She rises.*)

Teddy Come on, we've had a few laughs.

Trish Teddy, we haven't even *smiled*. Not for years. Still, no hard feelings –

Trish kisses Teddy lightly on the head.

– God, you reek of whisky – I'll leave this evening. I'll take the little car. I can never park the Jag . . .

Teddy Where are you going?

Trish What's it matter?

Lucille comes in from the hall. She has also tidied up a bit since we last saw her and has changed her dress for one of Trish's.

* **Lucille** Eh voilà . . . C'est pas mal? (*She twirls.*)

Trish Oh, ça vous va bien. Ça vous va mieux qu'à moi.

Lucille Je vous la renverrai par la poste.

Trish Ce n'ai pas la peine. Je n'en aurai plus besoin où je vais . . .

Lucille Vous allez où?

Trish Je quitte mon marie. Je vais habiter à Londres.

Teddy (*muttering*) Nyong, nyong, nyong, nyong, nyong . . .

Lucille À Londres? Vous avez un amant là-bas?

---

* **Lucille** Here I am at last . . . Does it look alright? (*She twirls.*)

Trish Oh, that suits you. Looks better than it does on me.

Lucille I'll post it back to you.

Trish Oh, there's no need. I shan't need it again where I'm going . . .

Lucille Where are you going?

Trish I'm leaving my husband. I'm going to live in London.

Teddy (*muttering*) Nyong, nyong, nyong, nyong, nyong . . .

Lucille London? You've got a lover there?

* Trish Non, seulement une soeur.

Lucille Oh, pauvre Teddy . . .

Trish Oui, pauvre Teddy. Vous pourriez peut-être passer un jour pour lui remonter le moral.

Lucille D'accord, à mon retour de clinique. Dites-lui que je m'arrêterai pour prendre un verre avec lui . . .

Teddy Is anyone allowed in on this bloody conversation or have I got to wait for the subtitles . . .?

Trish Lucille says, poor old you and she'll look in on her way back from her clinic and have a drink with you.

Teddy Jolly good.

† Lucille (*kissing Trish extravagantly*) Au revoir, Trish. Et bonne chance dans votre nouvelle vie . . .

Trish Merci . . . Teddy va vous accompagner à votre voiture . . .

Lucille Ah, Teddy . . .

Teddy I'll see you to your car. I'm seeing her to her car. You'll be here when I get back?

Trish Possibly.

Teddy No, hang on. We need to talk about this some more, Trish . . .

---

* **Trish** No, no. Just a sister.

Lucille Oh, poor Teddy . . .

Trish Yes, poor Teddy. Maybe you can look in and cheer him up.

Lucille I will. On my way back from the clinic. Tell him I'll stop by and have a drink with him . . .

† **Lucille** (*kissing Trish extravagantly*) Good-bye, Trish. Good luck in your new life . . .

Trish Thank you . . . Teddy will see you to your car . . .

105

Trish Not really, we don't.

Teddy I also need to know where everything's kept. No, don't go. For God's sake, don't go till I come back . . .

Lucille (*on the terrace*) Au revoir . . .

Trish Au revoir . . .

Teddy and Lucille go off to the garden.

(*to the picture*) No, sorry, Cat, this one's breaking with tradition, I'm afraid. She's getting out while she can still walk.

She goes to leave and nearly collides with Sally, who is in her dressing gown and looking very mournful.

Oh. Nice bath?

Sally nods.

Aren't you getting dressed again?

Sally shakes her head.

Bit early for bed, isn't it? Not even six o'clock.

Sally sits, gloomily.

Don't you want me to go, now? An hour ago you told me I should.

Sally (*muttering*) I don't care.

Trish Well, thank you. It doesn't matter one way or the other, I take it?

Sally Nothing I say's going to make any difference anyway, is it?

Trish Yes, it is. Of course it is. Do you want me to go or not?

Sally Yes. I don't want you to go but I think you should go. For your sake.

Trish You can come and see me in London. At Kirsty's. You're always looking for excuses to come to London, aren't you? You are. Oh, don't make this more difficult for me than it is already, Sally. Please.

Sally I don't think I want to go to London any more.

Trish Why not?

Sally I don't belong in London. I belong down here. I'm an ignorant, bumptious, stupid country lump. Like everyone else.

Trish Oh, for God's sake. What are you talking about, stupid? At school you're streets ahead of anyone, you're captain of this and head of that –

Sally I'm a tiny little fish in a minuscule puddle, that's all –

Trish Oh, I'm not talking to you when you're like this. Everything I say is wrong.

Sally Well, it's true, isn't it?

Trish (*angrily*) It is not true. And what's more, if you listened to yourself, you'd realise what an arrogant thing that is to say. Because it implies that everyone other than you is *incredibly* stupid. And if that is genuinely what you believe, Sally, then I promise you, you are in for a very rough ride indeed. Because although you are extremely bright and I'm terribly proud of you, as you go on you are going to meet lots and lots of people who are equally as bright as you and some, dare I say it, who are even brighter. And if you continue to look down your nose at the rest of the human race and don't show it a little more respect then all I can say is you're in for one hell of a life, darling. Now, please excuse me, I'm going to pack a suitcase.

Trish stamps out. Sally sits unhappily. In a moment she starts to cry. Jake comes on to the terrace with his briefcase. He stops when he sees Sally, considers what to do, then goes off again and comes back whistling noisily. Sally hastily pulls herself together.

Jake Hi.

Sally Hallo. You're very cheerful.

Jake Yes. Sorry.

A silence.

You're very gloomy.

Sally What do you want?

Jake I – er – I came to apologise, really.

Sally What for?

Jake This morning. In the garden. I read your private poem and I shouldn't have done, I'm just very sorry. You had every right to be angry with me.

Sally I was angry because you'd obviously been through my briefcase, that's all.

Jake Well, actually, I hadn't, but I can understand that you might think I had. So – anyway – here to make amends – (*He hold out his briefcase.*)

Sally What's this?

Jake My briefcase. I brought it so you could go through my briefcase.

Sally (*smiling, despite herself*) Really . . .

Jake Go on.

Sally No, I don't want to. Don't be silly.

Jake No, take it. Please. Please.

Sally takes the briefcase reluctantly.

Now open it. Go on. Snoop through everything, I don't mind . . .

Sally I'm really not –

Jake Please. Please.

Sally sighs and opens the briefcase. She stares at the contents, then lifts out a single red rose.

Sally What's this?

Jake It's for you.

Sally Thank you.

Jake I got it from the flower stall. At the fête.

Sally Yes. Thanks very much.

Jake Secondly . . .

Sally What?

Jake I think we should – we should – both go out somewhere tonight . . .

Sally No, Jake, honestly . . .

Jake . . . I don't care what we do, but I think we should go somewhere, the pub, the disco, a drive, a walk, it doesn't matter . . .

Sally . . . I don't think I could face . . .

Jake . . . because it's now half past five and, after all that's happened to us today, if you sit around here on your own till bedtime you're going to be suicidal. We both are. Let's face it.

Sally (*after a slight pause*) Yes, you're quite right.

Jake (*slightly surprised*) Good.

Sally (*getting up*) I'll get dressed. Come back in an hour for me.

Jake Right. Great.

Sally moves to the door. She has forgotten her rose.

Er – thirdly . . .

Sally What?

Jake Thirdly, I have something else to tell you.

Sally Yes?

Jake I – I – (*giving up*) – I'll tell you later on.

Sally (*smiling*) Alright. (*She goes out through the hall door.*)

Jake (*furious with himself*) Why can't you say it, you pillock? I love you. That's all it is. I love you. I love you. I love you. I love –

Sally has come back. Jake breaks off embarrassed.

Sally Forgot my rose. (*She picks up the rose and makes to go out again.*)

Jake I love you.

Sally What?

Jake I love you. I love you.

Sally I – I – (*Sally looks at him. She looks at her rose. She looks at Jake again. Today, it is all too much for her. She starts to cry and runs out through the door.*)

Jake (*despairingly*) Now what did I do? I'll never understand women. I know I won't. I'll never understand them . . . never . . .

Jake goes out. Trish comes in through the dining room doors with her suitcase.

Trish (*as she enters*) And another thing you – (*seeing the empty room*) Oh. (*She stands for a moment, holding her case, looks around her. As if making her final decision. Decisively*) Yes. Yes. (*to the room, the portrait, the house in general, resignedly*) Ah, well. That's life, I suppose.

> *Trish goes out into the hall. In a moment the front door slams.*
> *The lights fade to:*
> *Blackout.*

GARDEN

Characters

Teddy Platt, a businessman
Trish Platt, his wife, a designer
Sally Platt, their daughter, a schoolgirl
Giles Mace, a doctor
Joanna Mace, his wife, a teacher
Jake Mace, their son, a student reporter
Gavin Ryng-Mayne, a novelist
Barry Love, a shopkeeper
Lindy, his wife, a shopkeeper
Lucille Cadeau, an actress
Fran Briggs, her driver
Warn Coucher, a gardener
Izzie Truce, a housekeeper
Pearl Truce, an occasional cleaner
Several children of about seven or eight years old

Scene: the lower meadow area of the garden.

Time: a Saturday in August between eight o'clock in the morning and six in the evening.

Act One

SCENE ONE

Saturday, August 14th, 8.00 a.m.

Part of the garden of the house, known as the Lower Meadow. It is reached from the terrace at the back of the house via a more formal garden and then down a flight of stone steps.

The area is not quite as informal as perhaps its name suggests but merely the lower part of a much larger garden which has been allowed to grow wild. As a reminder of this, in the middle there is a murky looking, overgrown stone pond with a central fountain which long ago ceased to function.

The remaining area is rather flat and uneventful, surrounded by bushes with the odd gap for a pathway. However, shortly, this is the place where the full paraphernalia of an English garden fête will be assembled and erected: trestle tables, tents, stalls, side-shows and roped-off areas intended for special displays including, in this case, children's Maypole and adult Morris dancing.

It is long past dawn but the place still has an air of peace, not yet shattered by human intrusion. Birds are in full song. The sky is unsettled. Later, it could well rain.

In a moment, Joanna, a woman in her late thirties, tense and anxious and behaving decidedly suspiciously, enters. She looks nervously towards the house, hesitates and then, hearing someone coming, hurriedly hides in the bushes.

Joanna (*obviously finding this rather painful*) Aaah! Ooooh!

Warn, the gardener, enters along one of the paths with a barrow. He is probably in his late fifties or early

*sixties but he is not a man whose age is easy to assess.
He stops, rests the barrow and stares at the sky.*

(softly, from the depths of the bushes, in some discomfort)
Ah! Ah!

*Warn hears this and glances incuriously in Joanna's
direction. He is evidently well used to hearing strange
noises from bushes. He is about to set off again when
Izzie enters. She is a woman of about Warn's age
(whatever that is), stern faced and unsmiling. Someone
who feels her lot to be less than a happy one.*

Izzie There you are, then.

Warn grunts.

(handing him a small Tupperware box) Brought your
'levenses. You got 'em early. I'm busy today. Going to
rain, you reckon?

Warn looks at the sky and sucks his teeth.

Wash out the garden fête then, won't it? Shame that.
Rained last year, didn't it? Rains every year.

Warn reflects on this.

One thing. Keep her out of trouble anyway. I'm not
having it again this year, Warn. I'm not having it. She
monkeys about again in that little tent of hers, I warned
her. I won't be questionable . . . Fortune tellin' she calls
it. Fortune tellin'! Bloody Gypsy Rose with half her arse
showing.

Warn looks at the sky again.

Fortune's not in her face, wherever else. No, I won't have
it this year. I won't have it . . . She's a pyromaniac, that
girl. She needs a father, Warn, before she runs out of
control completely . . . Thirty years old next February.
Time she had a father.

Warn stares at the grass.

We got to do it right by her, Warn. What's past is past, I'm telling you. No use crying over spilt milk, it's all flowed under the bridge, now. You think about it.

Another little squeak from Joanna.

What's that, then? That them? Them, innit? What they up to in there? Grown people in bushes. Patricia I feel sorry for. She wouldn't be found dead in no bushes. Trying to smile like it ain't happening. Whole village knows, doesn't it? Not right for her. Admiral's daughter she were. She were bred for better.

They think about this.

No, they're shameless, those two. Like rhinos in rut. Teacher? She's more like a prostitute. Wouldn't have no child of mine taught by her. Not that Pearl needs much teaching. Well, I told her, she misbehaves today, she'll feel my restitution, I'm warning her. I'll bring your lunch down later, alright?

Izzie goes off. Warn looks after her for a second.

Warn (*tossing the sandwich box into his barrow, muttering*) Bloody women.

Warn goes off with his barrow. As he goes, the sound of a large dog barking in the distance and the sound of a man's voice.

Teddy (*off*) SPOOF! Will you stop that racket at once! Now, come on! Come on! Good boy! Come here, Spoof! Fetch, Spoof! Fetch the stick, boy! Gooooood boy, Spoof.

Renewed barking from Spoof.

Spoof, will you come back here at once, you bloody stupid animal. Right! That's it. I'm putting you down this time. That's your lot. This time I'm having you put down.

> *Teddy finally enters, a rather red faced man in his forties. He is wearing old clothes and boots.*
> *Spoof meantime, from his barking, appears to have made his way to the far side of Joanna's hiding place in the bushes.*
> *Some low growling.*

Spoof! Come on, boy. What you found, boy? You found a rabbit, boy?

> *More growling and a squeal from Joanna.*

What the hell have you got in there?

> *Joanna comes out of the bushes, hurriedly.*

Joanna (*to the dog in the bushes*) Get off! Get off me! (*recovering*) My God, that bloody dog! Look what it's done to my trousers. Can't you control it at all, Teddy?

Teddy Your own fault, you shouldn't hide in bushes. He mistook you for wild life. He's a hunter. Those dogs were originally bred for hunting. Basic instinct. He scents something in a bush, he'll flush it out.

Joanna Lethal.

Teddy What were you doing in there, anyway?

Joanna Hiding.

Teddy Hiding?

Joanna From your gardener.

Teddy Warn? He wouldn't say anything.

Joanna He was with that housekeeper of yours.

Teddy Izzie. Ah, yes. You'd do well to avoid her. The other one's alright.

Joanna Pearl? Is he still living with both of them?

Teddy Apparently.

Joanna I can't believe it. Even in this village. Do they all . . . you know? In the same bed?

Teddy Don't ask me, I just pay him to dig. I don't enquire. I pay him to dig, her to housekeep and the daughter to meander round the house breaking things as far as I can gather . . . (*seeing someone approaching along one of the paths, softly*) Look out. (*loudly*) No, these are *gregarious maximosa* with the bigger flowers but with the much smaller leaves . . .

Joanna (*loudly*) Oh, how interesting . . .

Jake, about nineteen years old, has entered. He is shy and slightly nervous. Seeing Teddy and Joanna, he smiles awkwardly.

Teddy (*to Jake*) 'Morning.

Joanna Hallo, Jake.

Jake (*embarrassed*) Hi, Mum.

Joanna I thought you were having a lie-in this morning?

Jake No, I have to – I have some things . . . You know.

Joanna Right. Mr – Teddy was just showing me these interesting shrubs.

Jake Oh, yes. Great. Right. Well. See you later.

Joanna Yes.

Teddy Cheerio, Jake.

Jake Dad's just . . . in the kitchen. Having breakfast.

Joanna Oh, good.

Jake goes off. They watch him go.

(*quieter*) He definitely knows.

Teddy Well . . .

Joanna He does, he definitely does. Which means Sally must know.

Teddy Not necessarily.

Joanna Obviously. They're . . . good friends. Jake will have told Sally – assuming she doesn't already know anyway. And then Sally will have told her mother. She'll have told Trish . . .

Teddy Not necessarily . . .

Joanna Daughters always tell their mothers everything . . .

Teddy No, they don't . . .

Joanna I always tell my mother everything.

Teddy Have you told her about us?

Joanna No, don't be silly, of course I haven't.

Teddy There you are then.

Joanna The thought of Trish ever finding out . . . I couldn't face it. Giles doesn't know. I'm certain. But then he and Jake – all they ever talk about is football . . .

Teddy I'm glad about that. I mean, Giles and I, we go back a long – way. I think I'm practically his best friend, poor bloke . . .

Joanna (*keen to change the subject*) Well?

Teddy What?

Joanna You wanted to see me. Urgently, you said.

Teddy Yes. (*a sudden yell*) Spoof, you come off that! Off! Off! At once! You keep right away from there! Bad boy!

Joanna Shhh! Shhh!

Teddy Did you see that? He was trying to dig up that sapling. Most dogs are just content to pee on them. He has to dig the bloody things up first. (*to Spoof*) That's better. You sit there. Good boy. Yes, you eat that. (*to himself*) Whatever it is. Looks like someone's head.

Joanna I don't know how we can ever have secret meetings if you insist on bringing that dog along.

Teddy He's my alibi. Why else would I be wandering about at the crack of dawn? Anyway, he needs the exercise, poor bastard.

Joanna Wouldn't it be wonderful? Just once. To meet indoors. I just suddenly long for the great indoors for once. I mean, flat on my back in all these summer houses and potting sheds and gazebos and ditches. God, how could I ever face Giles if he found out? You know I've loved every minute of it, of course I have, but wouldn't it be lovely, Teddy, just for once, to lie together in clean sheets? We're getting a bit old, aren't we? Well, I am. I'm beginning to feel the wear and tear a bit, that's all . . . My back's playing up again – and then, the other day, when that bloody dog jumped on us . . . I mean, let's face it – we're not teenagers any more, are we?

Teddy Well, that was what I was . . . Listen. I'm glad, in a way, that you've said all that because . . . Erm. This will probably come as a relief, in that case. Erm. I had it all worked out. Erm. I think it's got to stop.

Joanna Stop?

Teddy 'Fraid so.

Joanna What has?

Teddy Us.

Pause.

Joanna You're joking.

Teddy No, I'm –

Joanna You're ditching me?

Teddy Not really. I'm –

Joanna Just like that? I can't believe it. You're joking? Teddy, please tell me you're joking.

Teddy I'm sorry, from what you were just saying just now, I thought perhaps it might have been a relief . . .

Joanna What have I done? Is it me? Tell me what I've done.

Teddy You haven't done anything, Jo. It's not you. Not at all, it's not you. It's just – things are getting a bit out of hand.

Joanna With Trish? You mean with Trish?

Teddy Partly, but –

Joanna Sally has told her, I knew it. Trish does know.

Teddy No, she doesn't. I swear she doesn't. At least I don't think she does.

She is on the verge of breaking up.

Jo . . .

Joanna Listen, Teddy, I didn't mean all those things. I'm perfectly happy with sheds, I really am. I was only just saying that . . .

Teddy Jo, I – (*yelling*) Spoof, will you put that down at once! (*softly again, to her*) – it's just that circumstances have altered, you see, Jo.

But Joanna is now a limp rag of misery.

Joanna Tell me what I have to do, Teddy. What I can do to get you back. I'll do anything. I'll change. Whatever you want . . .

Teddy No, no. Really, you don't want to do that. Don't change a hair. It's me. I'm just a bastard who's walking away. I'm not worthy of you, Jo. I'm a worthless womaniser. (*getting quite angry with himself*) A selfish, egotistic, self-centred, licentious, egocentric bastard. God! Sometimes I get so filled with self-loathing . . .

Joanna Ssshhh. You're none of those things. You're a wonderful lover. I couldn't bear it if you stopped making love to me. You've brought me alive again, Teddy. I was dead. You've brought me back to life . . .

Teddy (*a trifle alarmed*) Don't talk like that, Jo. You make me sound like some bloody faith-healer. Forget all about me. Put me out of your mind, Jo, out of your life.

Joanna How can I?

Teddy It's the only way . . .

Joanna We're all supposed to be having lunch together today, anyway.

Teddy Oh God, are we?

Joanna It's the garden fête.

Teddy Oh, yes. Of course.

Joanna Maybe we could live like your gardener does? All together in the same house? You, me and Trish, all together . . .?

Teddy No, I don't honestly think that's a frightfully good idea, Jo.

Joanna I wouldn't mind. I've no pride.

Teddy No, but I don't think that sort of thing would be Trish's bag. Not at all. Listen, I've got to get back, Jo. I'm sorry.

Joanna (*in a tiny voice*) Will I see you tonight? Can we meet tonight?

Teddy (*gently*) Best not, Jo. Really. (*He takes her hand.*) Really and truly.

Joanna removes her hand from his and gives a little whimper.

OK? Listen, I'm afraid I've got this meeting with . . . someone important. In a minute.

Joanna (*as small as can be*) Go. Go on, then.

Teddy See you . . . see you around. At lunchtime, I suppose. We'll both just have to put on a – brave face, won't we? Yes.

They stand for a second. She frozen in her misery; he with nothing more to say.

I really hate to leave you like this. (*Another pause.*) Must get Warn to fix that fountain, you know. There's a blockage somewhere. That's all it is, I'm certain. I remember as a kid, it used to look quite spectacular . . . Yes. (*suddenly yelling*) Spoof! Come on then, boy. Come on!

Barking from Spoof.

Biscuit! Let's go and get a biscuit! That's a good boy! Away you go!

Spoof's barking recedes rapidly.

And keep off that, you stupid dog. How many more times?

*Teddy goes off after Spoof, back towards the house.
Joanna left alone can contain it no longer. She lets out
a terrible wail of grief and sinks to her knees. In time,
Warn returns with his barrow, now empty. He passes
Joanna without appearing to notice her and goes off
again. She continues to cry. In a moment, Pearl enters.
She is as different from her mother, Izzie, as it is
possible to be. In her late twenties, lithe and attractive.
She carries a small container with another snack for
Warn.*

    *She stops when she sees Joanna, hesitates and then
comes and sits down near her. She says nothing for a
moment. Joanna notices her and then chooses to
ignore her.*

Pearl (*at length*) Be a feller then, will it?

    Joanna looks at her.

Yes. It'll be a feller. The only bugger make you cry like
that'll be a feller.

    Pause. Pearl reflects.
    Joanna stares at her, rather startled.

No offence? Don't mind me saying, do you?

Joanna (*faintly*) No. Thank you.

Pearl Got a good bloke there. That one. Mind my
saying? (*indicating towards Teddy and the house*) Not
him. T'other one. Your husband. You ought to try and
hang on to him. Good bloke, he is.

Joanna (*beginning to have heard enough*) Yes, thank
you.

Pearl Good doctor an' all. Some of 'em don't give a
stuff. But my friend's kid, he sat up all night with her.
Terrible fever. All night. Not many do that. Not on the
National bloody Health, they don't.

Warn enters. He has an oily rag and a dip-stick in his hands.

Hallo, here he comes. Better give the bugger his elevenses, then. All else fails, feed 'em, eh? (*She laughs.*) Eh? Eh?

Joanna smiles faintly.

There you are. Looking for you.

Warn (*to Joanna*) Be there long, are you?

Joanna Sorry? Oh. Do you want me to move? I'll move. Sorry.

Pearl Warn'll be wantin' to mow.

Joanna Yes, of course. Mow. You'll be wanting to mow, won't you? For this afternoon for the fête. I'll move, don't worry. I'll move . . .

Pearl 'Less you want to get mowed.

Joanna (*laughing feebly*) Yes.

Pearl Cheaper than waxing 'em. (*She laughs.*) You alright, then?

Joanna Yes. Thank you. I'm fine. Yes. I know precisely what I have to do now. Precisely. Thank you. (*She starts to move off down one of the paths.*)

As Joanna goes out, Giles, her husband comes from that same direction in something of a hurry. He is a pleasant, affable if somewhat ineffectual man in his thirties.

Giles Hallo, darling. What are you doing here?

Joanna Nothing, I was just . . .

Giles You alright?

Joanna Fine.

Giles You look a bit . . .

Joanna No. (*She goes off.*)

Giles (*to the others*) She gets this terrible hay-fever. My colleague prescribed these drops but she never takes them. (*He laughs.*) Typical.

> Warn and Pearl stare at him impassively.
> Giles gets a little embarrassed.

Think it might hold off. The rain. Don't you? Hope so. (*He feels the ground.*) Pretty firm. Pretty firm. Take a bit of spin. (*He laughs.*) No, I was thinking underfoot. We've got the Morris dancing team today. We're doing a little display. Usually quite popular. I think people enjoy it. I think they do. All part of our common cultural and social heritage. Unites us all in a funny way. Rich and poor, young and old. Great leveller, the dance. Don't you think?

Pearl Bit of a laugh.

Giles (*loath to argue*) Well . . . possibly, yes. Got the Maypole too, this year. Really branching out. That's my wife's project. Joanna's been rehearsing them for weeks. Some of her class, that is. I saw a rehearsal the other night. I think they've really got into the swing of it. Try and catch it, if you can. See what you think. I think you'll be impressed.

> Pearl and Warn don't look greatly enthused.

Well, must get on. Excuse me. (*as he goes*)

> Giles has gone off towards the house. Warn belches.

Pearl He's alright. Poor bloke. She don't know when she's well off. I'd have him. She don't want him, I'd take him off her hands. Bit borin' but not a bad looker. Being a doctor, could be useful, too. Like being married to a plumber. If you spring a leak, he'll fix it for you.

Warn is feeling the grass and looking at the sky again.

Here. Brought you your 'levenses. Busy today. Got all
them people coming to lunch. Doing me silver service.
I nearly got it off. 'Less we have sprouts. I'm all over the
place with bloody sprouts. I can do carrots. If they're cut
long, you know. And beans. I'm alright with beans now.
I've mastered beans. Runner beans. Not them broad
buggers, they're right bastards. I had 'em everywhere last
time. We were pickin' them up for months. I don't know
why they don't bung it all on the plate and have done
with it. Like normal people.

Warn is studying the fountain now.

Mum's on the warpath. Been on at me all day. We better
not do nothing this year, Warn. She'll be watching us.
She can get right barmy, you know that. Like when she
went at us with that hot iron, you remember. Bloody
lucky it were still plugged in, it could have killed us.
Remember? First time she caught us in bed together.
Remember? (*She laughs.*) That was a laugh. Still, that
were before. It's different now. Circumstances have
changed. That's all I'm saying. Know what I mean?

Warn appears not to know nor care.

I mean, I don't care. Don't matter to me. I never ask
anything of anyone. Liberty Hall, I am. But my mum,
she . . . Well, anyway. You suit yourself. Be nice to get it
settled though, wouldn't it? Get a bit of peace then. You
suit yourself, though. It's between you and Mum.
Nothing to do with me. I'm easy. I don't care. (*A silence.
She reckons she's pursued this tricky topic as much as
she can.*) Bloody garden fetes, eh? Bet you're looking
forward to it, in't yer? In't yer? You love 'em, don't you?
Eh? Make your bloody year, don't they? All your lawns
churned up. People parking all over your verges. Bloody
pig got loose last year, remember? Dug up half the

bloody veg. I hope we have that army again, they're alright. Big lads shooting each other every which way. Nuclear war they'd be off like bloody rabbits, wouldn't they?

Warn sniffs noisily.

Got a film star today. French one. She were in a film. *The Unex . . . Unin . . . Uninspiring . . .* I don't know. I never seen it. She gets blown up early on. Deirdre told me. But she's good while she lasts. You ought to clean this pond out. It's disgustin'. Breeding ground for things is this. You want to get a stick and clean it out.

Sally and Jake appear, coming from the house. Sally is Trish and Teddy's only child. Seventeen and still at school, she is a serious, sometimes rather intense girl who has recently grown very concerned with Life and The World. She is wearing her school uniform and carries a briefcase.

Sally (*calling as they enter*) Pearl, Izzie's looking for you.

Pearl Oh, right, Sally. Thank you.

Sally It seems there's something you haven't yet done that you're supposed to have done . . .

Pearl Yes, I'll go and do it. Be my hooverin', I expect. (*Pearl hurries back to the house.*)

Sally Alright, Warn?

Warn grunts.

Ready for the invasion this afternoon? Don't blame me. Blame my mother.

Warn nods and goes off.

I always say there's nothing can set you up more for the day than a good conversation with Warn.

Jake They were standing just over there.

Sally I see.

Jake Quite close together. Pretending to look at the shrubbery. Your father was pretending to show my mother the shrubbery.

Sally Oh.

Jake He hadn't even bothered to learn the right names.

Sally Well. At least they were both standing up.

Jake (*gloomily*) Just.

Sally There's nothing we can do, Jake. I've said. If they don't want to talk about it, what can we do? I know what I'd like to do. Get them all together in one room, sit them down and say come on, you stupid lot, now sort yourselves out. But somehow I don't think that's going to happen because that's not the way they do things.

Jake I just hope my dad never finds out. He's such a – he's a really decent guy, you know, he really is. He's devoted to Mum, it would just – destroy him . . .

Sally Perhaps he's tougher than you think, Jake. People can surprise you sometimes.

Jake I still don't understand why Mum . . . I mean, no disrespect to your father, but . . .

Sally Say what you like about him, I don't care . . .

Jake My dad's so . . . he's got this incredible faith in people. He trusts. He's always determined to find the good side. You hear him reading the paper in the morning. (*in a fair impersonation of Giles*) 'Oh, I don't think this man really meant to cut his wife's throat, you know. He was probably showing her his new razor, that's all.' It's amazing in someone of his age, really.

Most people by then are – eaten up with mistrust and cynicism, aren't they? He's somehow survived all that.

Sally Must be nice to love your parents . . .

Jake Don't you love your mother?

Sally Sometimes. Sometimes she drives me up the wall. Like now. Why won't she talk about it? She knows. We all know she knows. Yet she behaves as if it isn't happening.

Jake Her way of coping.

Sally Well, maybe. But it's very tough on the rest of us. On me. (*after a slight pause*) Tell me, do you think I'm . . .?

Jake What?

Sally Nothing. Just something someone said.

Jake You're what?

Sally Selfish. Do you think I'm a selfish person?

Jake No.

Sally You don't think I take advantage of people? Use them?

Jake No, I don't think so. Not at all.

Sally No, I don't, either. It's rubbish, isn't it? Parents talk utter rubbish sometimes, don't they? They give birth to you and as you grow up they immediately start reading themselves into you – whether they're there or not. It starts innocently enough with innocuous physical features – oh, look she's got my nose, isn't that sweet? – but it finishes up, oh, look she's got all your megalomania, isn't that terrible? It's guilt, that's all. I am selfish therefore surely you must be selfish as well.

Jake Possibly.

Sally You got a lot on this morning?

Jake (*eagerly*) No, why?

Sally Good. Then you can wait for me at the school and bring me back if you like.

Jake (*unfazed*) Sure. I've got nothing till this afternoon. Till my interview with Madame Lucille Cadeau.

Sally Oh yes, of course. Ace Mace, Boy Reporter. Big deal.

Jake She's the best bit in the movie actually. It's a pity she gets blown up so early on . . .

Sally (*as they start to go*) Been dreaming about her, have you?

Jake No, of course not . . .

* **Sally** Je suis à vous pour toujours, mam'selle. Je vous aime. Prenez-moi, je suis à vous.

Jake Oh, Sally, knock it off . . .

Sally Embrassez-moi, mon amour. Prenez mon corps et faites-en ce que vous désirez. Je suis votre esclave pour toujours, ma chère Lucille, mon amour . . .

Jake Oh, Sally . . .

Sally Got your notebook?

Jake Yes.

Sally Inside your Ace Mace briefcase . . .?

---

* **Sally** I am yours for ever, mam'selle. I love you. Take me I am yours.

Jake Oh, Sally, knock it off . . .

Sally Kiss me, my love. Take my body and use it as you desire. I am your slave for ever, my dearest Lucille, my love . . .

Jake Give it a break. It's just till I go to college that's all . . .

They have both gone. Their voices continue into the distance. Silence.
Somewhere nearby, a motor mower starts up, splutters briefly and dies.

Warn (*off*) Ah, you bugger!

Trish, a woman in her forties whose soft English beauty has only very faintly faded, comes on from the direction of the house. She is wearing her gardening gloves and carries some roses she has just cut with her secateurs.

Trish (*calling*) Warn, I've just taken some of these for the table, alright? (*She listens. To herself*) Yes? I think that sounds like a yes. Jolly good.

A guttural mumbling from Warn.
Another failed attempt to start the mower. Another muffled oath.

(*to herself*) Dear God. He'll rupture himself. We must get a new mower. Or a new gardener.

Joanna appears. She has changed her clothes, pulled herself together and now looks pale and determined. She stops as she sees Trish. She takes a deep breath.

Joanna Oh. Trish . . .

Trish turns and sees her for the first time.

Trish Jo. Hallo . . .

Joanna Trish . . .

Trish How are you today? Feeling any better?

Joanna Better?

Trish Yes, haven't you had terribly bad hay-fever? Someone was saying. Giles, probably.

Joanna Trish . . .

Trish I think it'll stay fine . . .

Joanna Trish.

Trish The forecast says rain . . .

Joanna I have something to say to you.

Trish . . . but then they're always getting it wrong, aren't they?

Joanna Patricia, please.

Trish Mmm?

Joanna I have something to say to you. To tell you. It is something I would give anything in the world not to have to tell you, I would cut off both my arms rather than tell you, but you need to be told. I can't live with myself for another minute unless I do tell you.

Trish Oh, dear.

Joanna Sit down.

They sit.

Yet now I've decided to tell you, I don't know quite how to put it into words . . .

Trish You and Teddy are fucking each other.

Joanna (*on the brink of tears*) Yes.

Trish There. That wasn't so difficult, was it?

The sound of the mower starting, spluttering, stopping again and Warn's muffled oath.

Joanna How did you know?

Trish (*impatiently*) Oh, come *on* . . . Credit me with some intelligence, Jo, for God's sake. Between you, you've flattened every bloody bush in the garden cavorting around . . .

Joanna (*starting to cry again*) That's not true . . .

Trish Every flower bed's imprinted with your wretched rear end. I don't mind, Jo, I really don't – not that it would make a blind bit of difference if I did mind – but, no, I don't give a tinsel fairy's fart what you do – but just don't come snivelling to me when Teddy decides to dump you, as he obviously has done. You want a shoulder to cry on, find someone else's. Alright?

Joanna (*after a slight pause*) Do you really hate me, Trish?

Trish No. I don't hate you. Frankly, I think you're a very, very stupid woman, Jo, but then I've always thought that, even before all this.

Joanna I am, I am . . .

Trish God knows how you manage to teach anyone . . .

Joanna They're only five-year-olds . . .

Trish They've still got to be brighter than you. Oh, do blow your nose . . .

Joanna (*fumbling for her tissues*) What's going to happen?

Trish Well, you've had your romp. Now you have to face up to it all, don't you? That's how it works. You've told me. Now you'd better go and tell your husband.

Joanna (*horrified*) Giles? I couldn't tell Giles.

Trish Of course you must.

Joanna I couldn't, Trish, I just couldn't . . .

Trish Oh, Jo, for heaven's sake, woman . . .

Joanna You don't know him. It would kill him if he knew. He's the dearest, most trusting man in the world. He'd trust me with his life.

Trish Then he's an idiot as well, isn't he? Alright, if you won't tell him, I will.

Joanna No! No!

Trish Someone's got to tell him, Joanna. Otherwise it's only going to be left for him to find out for himself. Accidentally. Probably in the village pub. And that is definitely not the way. That is no way to treat anyone. Giles is up at our house now. I'll send him down to you. Wait here.

Joanna (*drawing back*) I can't. I just can't. I'm sorry.

Trish You have to. It's the price you pay. Don't go away. See you at lunchtime. And I expect you there, Jo. You can wreck my marriage but I'll never forgive you if you ruin my luncheon party.

> *Trish marches off towards the house in determined fashion, still carrying her roses and secateurs. Joanna stares after her, dismayed.*

Joanna (*feebly to Trish's retreating back*) Trish . . . Trish . . . Oh God!

> *The sound of the mower bursting into life again. Once again, it rapidly dies with a splutter.*

Warn (*off, in a fury*) Bloody bastard bollocking bitch bugger . . .

> *Joanna stares, startled for a moment, then plunges back into her own welter of self-pity.*

Joanna Giles . . . there's something you have to know . . . I've had this meaningless fling . . . it meant nothing . . . it was just . . . animal lust . . .

Warn has come stamping across.

Joanna attempts to cover the fact that she has been caught talking to herself by singing.

(*lamely, for Warn's benefit*) Diddly-diddly-dee . . .

Warn ignores her, involved as he is in his own private battle, man and machine. He goes off.

(*trying again*) It was just an affair. For God's sake, Giles. A silly old affair. What's so special about it . . .? (*frustratedly*) Oh . . . (*She stares up at an overhanging tree branch. She takes off her scarf wondering if it's long enough to hang herself. It isn't. Trying again*) Giles, I've reached that stage in life when I'm at a cross-roads . . . Teddy just happened to be the one who was standing by the signpost . . . it could have been anyone, Giles . . . it could have . . .

She breaks off again as Warn returns with an oil can. She smiles weakly at him. He ignores her.

(*trying again when he's gone*) He swept me off my feet, Giles, I was particularly vulnerable. Unsure. A woman needs constant reassurance, Giles, you must understand that . . . She has to be told occasionally that she's still – desirable . . .

Warn's mower roars into life once more. This time, instead of dying, the engine catches and roars some more.

Warn (*off, in triumph*) Whey-hey! There you goes, you bugger!

Joanna is only dimly aware of this. She is now at the fountain. She steps on to the rim and gazes into the depths.

Joanna (*trying again*) I've been a complete and utter fool. Forgive me, my darling. If you want to hit me,

I'll quite understand . . . but what I need more than anything in the world is for you to take me in your arms and try and forgive . . . try and forgive your stupid, foolish wife . . . (*She is about to jump. She loses her balance and slips, one foot going into the water, then the other. She stands in about eight inches of water. Feeling somewhat foolish*) Oh.

> *Warn returns, punching the air briefly in triumph, and crosses the garden. He sees Joanna and looks at her sourly. Joanna, aware of him, laughs feebly. Warn goes.*

(*trying again, still standing in the water, in a baby voice*) Gilesy . . . Jo-Jo's been a silly girl . . . (*Joanna steps out of the pond in her sopping shoes, squelching slightly. She cries softly. She, too, starts up the terrace steps. As she does so, trying again*) Jake, I wonder if you could possibly pass on a message to your father . . .

> *She reaches the terrace and gazes over the upstage parapet, contemplating the drop. Below her, the unseen mower chugs merrily on.*

(*turning sharply away from the prospect and trying again*) Dear Giles, by the time you read this letter, I shall be far away. Don't try to find me, my darling . . . Oh, God.

> *She takes courage and climbs on to the parapet.*
> *Warn re-enters with a signpost reading* TO THE HOME FARM. *He climbs the steps staring down at the lawn, inspecting it, and failing to notice Joanna. As he draws level with her, Joanna gives another little cry.*

Oh . . .

> *Warn turns slightly at the sound, inadvertently clipping Joanna with the end of the signpost and knocking her off the parapet.*

(*as she falls*) Aaaaah!

A crash as she lands on the mower. The engine roars briefly and dies with a final splutter.
Silence. A plume of smoke rises above the parapet.
Warn, incredulous and speechless, walks to the parapet edge and looks over.
From below, a moan from Joanna.
Giles enters from the house.

Giles What is it? What's happening? Warn? What's going on?

Giles joins Warn and looks over the parapet.

(*very alarmed*) Jo? Jo?

Another groan from Joanna.

Are you alright? Warn, what happened to her?

Warn Bloody women! (*He sets off again with his signpost, furious.*)

Giles (*hurrying down the steps*) Wait there, darling! Don't try and move! Don't try and move!

Giles hurries down the steps.
As he reaches the bottom, Joanna stumbles on, battered, a little dazed and slightly oily.

(*stopping and looking at her, incredulously*) Jo . . . Jo . . .?

Joanna (*faintly*) Giles . . .

Giles (*moving to her*) What happened, darling? What is it? (*He makes to touch her.*)

Joanna (*drawing back*) Nooo.

Giles What?

Joanna Don't touch me . . . don't touch me . . .

Giles What?

Joanna . . . you mustn't touch me!

Giles What is it?

Joanna Giles, I . . . Giles, I . . . I've . . . I've been hoping . . . I've been trying . . . I've been wanting . . . I've been so . . . I've been . . . I've been . . .

Giles (*gently*) You've been what? You've been what, darling?

Joanna (*after a deep breath*) I've been having an affair with Teddy.

Giles (*taking this in by degrees*) You've been . . .? You've been . . .? You've been . . . Teddy?

Joanna (*tiny*) Yes.

Giles quite suddenly lets out the most terrible drawn out cry of despair and rushes off.

Giles (*as he goes*) Teddddddddyyyyyy!

Giles has gone.
Joanna walks a few paces as if to follow him. She stops. She is still in shock.

Joanna Oh.

Warn has entered with his sandwich box in one hand and the flattened grass bin from the mower in the other. He tosses the latter on to the ground disgustedly. He gives Joanna another glare. He then sits and starts to eat.
After a second, Joanna starts to totter off after Giles, whimpering softly as she does so, half in unhappiness, half in pain. Warn watches her till she goes.

Warn (*looking upwards at the sky*) Reckon we're in for a storm . . . the bugger.

*As Warn sits there, chewing contentedly, the lights fade
to:*
   Blackout.

SCENE TWO

Saturday, August 14th, 11.00 a.m.
   *The same. The grass, unsurprisingly, remains unmown.
It is still overcast. Pearl enters from the house. She has
another, slightly larger, sandwich box. She stops and
looks around.*

Pearl (*calling*) Warn! Warn! Lunch! Where you hiding,
then?

   *Pearl goes off in search of Warn. As she does so, from
   a different direction, Barry and Lindy Dove enter.
   They are in their thirties. He is undoubtedly the
   driving force behind the fête. Lindy loyally serves as
   his dogsbody and scapegoat. They stagger on, the first
   of many journeys they will make, carrying equipment
   for the forthcoming event – tents, bunting, ropes and
   poles to form enclosures, produce, etc.*

Barry (*as they enter*) . . . Right, that's it . . . come on,
come on . . . with me, with me, with me!

Lindy Yes, yes, yes . . .

Barry . . . and just here . . . one – two . . . huuup!

Lindy (*with him*) . . . huuup!

   *They set down their burden together, a well-rehearsed
   team. They stand, catching their breath.*

Whew! She's loaded down today, isn't she? She's loaded
down today is our Winnie . . .

Barry Certainly is. Right down on her axles. That's why I was driving so slowly . . .

Lindy Yes.

Barry Ready for the next?

Lindy So far so good with the weather.

Barry Thus far.

Lindy (*wagging her finger at the sky*) Don't you dare rain, do you hear me? Don't you dare!

> *Barry and Lindy go off.*
> *As they go, Warn has entered with a sign in one hand, inscribed* TO THE MAIN HOUSE.
> *He watches them with distaste.*
> *He glares at the small pile of gear on his grass.*
> *Pearl enters, still in search of him with her sandwich box.*

Pearl (*calling*) Oy!

> *Warn turns.*

There y'are. Brought your lunch.

> *Warn takes the box with a grunt.*

Is it you took down all them signs, then? It were, weren't it? It were you. You old bugger, you do it every year, don't you? Soon as the fête's here down come all the signs. Nobody can find their way in or out of the place. If I didn't know you better, Warn Coucher, I'd say you done that deliberate.

> *She examines the pile of stuff so far accumulated by Barry and Lindy.*

There's my little tent there. Look. You goin' to put it up for me? Well, long as someone does. I'll be laughing if it rains. Only one sittin' in the dry, won't I? I'll have queues round the block.

Warn is staring at the pile of stuff.

She's in a fury, my mum. Their dinner's spoilin' 'cause half of them are late. Probably 'cause you uprooted all the signs. They're all drivin' round the country looking for the main gates, I bet. Anyway, her dinner's spoilin'. She said by the time they arrive the beef will be indelible. (*laughing*) Indelible. Good one that. You get it? Indelible. Piss ignorant old bag, isn't she? See you later.

> *Pearl goes back to the house.*
> *Warn glares after her.*
> *Sally enters along one of the paths. She is in a fury. She hurls her briefcase on to the ground ahead of her. Jake trails unhappily along behind.*
> *Sally stops. Jake stops, too. They stand in silence. Warn stares at them and then goes off.*

Sally (*at length*) No, I'm sorry. I just cannot believe it.

Jake Right.

Sally How people can be so *thick*, so *dim*, so *stupid*, so *short-sighted*. It's unbelievable.

Jake Well . . .

Sally *Unbelievable.*

Jake I wasn't at the meeting, of course, but it certainly sounds as if –

Sally Those are supposedly mature, intelligent sixth-formers. The so-called cream of the school. God help us all! If they're incapable of listening to a rational proposal without screaming and banging tables –

Jake Some of them agreed with you, surely – ?

Sally How could they? I was never allowed to finish. I was just shouted down and then told to sit. As if I was a child of three. God, I'm so bloody angry. I'm going to resign. This time I'm going to resign, I really am.

145

Jake I wouldn't do that . . .

Sally See how they get on without me. See how far they get with Catriona Braithwaite . . . Good luck to them, I say. God, she's so *stupid*. (*mimicking, savagely, in a high whining voice*) 'I don't think we can possibly do that, Sally. It's against everything we stand for . . .'

> *Silence.*
> *Barry and Lindy return, this time with separate loads.*

Barry Good morning, Sally. Good morning, Jake.

Jake 'Morning.

Lindy Good morning.

Sally (*tersely*) 'Llo.

Barry (*to Lindy*) No, no, no, no, no, Lindy. Over there, dear. Over there.

Lindy Oh, I'm sorry.

Barry (*as he goes off again*) Do try and listen to me. Do try and listen, dear . . .

Lindy I was listening, dear, I was just . . .

Barry Saves a lot of time later if you listen, doesn't it?

Lindy (*cheerily, back to Sally*) Is it going to rain, that's the question?

Sally (*sourly*) Haven't a clue.

> *Barry and Lindy go off.*

Jake Well. Maybe you should resign, then.

Sally (*sharply*) What?

Jake I said, maybe you should resign . . .

Sally We can't just walk away from everything, Jake. Every time we feel –

Jake (*anxious not to incur her wrath*) No, no. Right.

  A silence between them.

What about this evening, then?

Sally Maybe I should resign. I don't know. Maybe you're right.

Jake Are we going out somewhere? Do you fancy going out?

Sally Not tonight.

Jake (*sadly*) OK. If you change your mind . . .

Sally Take someone else out, Jake.

Jake I don't want to take anyone else out.

  Barry comes on with Gavin. Gavin is in his late forties, urbane, charming, the ideal diplomat.

Barry I say, Sally, sorry could you possibly help, please? This gentleman's driven to the back gate by mistake. Could you possibly show him up to the house, do you think?

Gavin I'm so sorry. I got completely lost. There don't appear to be any signs.

Sally Aren't there? There's usually masses of them.

Barry I think Warn may have taken them down. He's cutting back the vegetation . . . I'll leave you, then.

Gavin (*to Barry*) Thank you, so much. You're very kind.

  Barry goes off.

Sally. Right?

Sally Yes, how did you . . .?

Gavin Gavin Ryng-Mayne with a Y. Gavin. Hallo. I think when we last met you were about six months old. I'm an old friend of your father's.

Sally Oh, right. Well, let me . . . How do you do? Follow me.

Gavin (*as they go*) Thank you. What a glorious place. I'd no idea . . .

Jake (*calling after them, rather slighted*) Hallo. I'm Jake, incidentally . . .

Gavin (*almost off*) Hallo, Jake! See you later, I hope.

> *Gavin and Sally have gone off towards the house. Jake, rather put out by this interruption, stands undecided.*
> *Barry and Lindy return carrying something between them. They are in the midst of one of their minor differences.*

Barry . . . I never said that . . .

Lindy . . . I think you did, dear . . .

Barry . . . I would never have said that . . .

Lindy Well, you said something like that . . .

Barry . . . I'm sorry, I would never have said anything remotely like that . . .

Lindy . . . Well, I wouldn't have made it up, would I?

> *They set down their load with the other things.*

Barry I don't know, do I? Frankly, Lindy, most of the time, I don't know what goes on in that head of yours . . .

Lindy You definitely said . . .

Barry I beg your pardon, I did not say that. I said *possibly*, that's all . . .

Lindy I don't remember any possibly . . .

They have gone off again. Jake sees Sally's briefcase which she has left. He picks it up. He holds it. It is unfastened. He goes to fasten it. Curiosity gets the better of him. He looks inside rather guiltily. He spies a sheet of paper. He pulls it out. It is a hand-written rough draft of a verse.

Jake (*reading*)
How can I ever hear a heart,
My head denies with such insistence?
How do I ever trust a heart,
Which doubt drowns out with such persistence?
How will I ever feel my heart,
Whilst caution proffers such resistance?
How could I ever give my heart,
When I deny its whole existence?

Giles enters from the house. He is deep in his own thoughts. Jake hurriedly replaces the paper and closes the briefcase.

Dad . . .

Giles Oh. Hallo, Jake. There you are. I was . . . Glad I caught you. I wanted to . . . Seen your mother this morning?

Jake Briefly.

Giles Right.

Pause.

How's things, then?

Jake Oh. You know.

Giles That your briefcase?

Jake No.

Giles No, I didn't think it was. Hadn't seen it before.

Jake It's Sally's.

Giles Uh-huh. How is she?

Jake Pretty well.

Giles Are things between you – moving along?

Jake No. Not really. Well, they're sort of moving but not going anywhere. If you know what I mean.

Giles Oh. I'm sorry to hear that.

Jake It's difficult, isn't it? Sometimes. To know if someone is telling you it's OK or to go away. You know. Women especially. They seem to . . . seem to . . . seem to . . . I don't know.

Giles This is Sally we're talking about?

Jake Yes. She gives you – she gives me different signals, you know. I think she likes me . . . sometimes she's really glad to see me . . . and it's really good between us. And then another time, it's like she puts the shutters up, you know. Doesn't want to know. I don't quite know what to do. I mean, half of me wants to say well, to hell with this, I'm off. But the other half of me . . . You know.

Giles Yes.

Jake I couldn't bear not to see her again.

Giles Ah. I know the problem.

Jake So. It's not a very happy time for me. At the moment. Pretty pathetic, just hanging around. Like a dog. I don't know – I don't – I don't know what to do for the best.

Giles Yes. It's never . . . never easy, Jake. I have to say. Well, for some people it seems to be but . . . People like you and me, I think we're probably rather the – rather the – rather the –

Jake The – the – same.

Giles Yes. I mean, with your mother, for instance . . . I wanted to talk about her actually, Jake. Talk about. Her.

Jake Yes?

Giles I have to tell you, Jake, I wish I could keep this from you but – you'll have to know sooner or later – Joanna's been having an affair.

Jake Yes.

Giles You knew?

Jake Yes. With Mr Platt.

Giles Ah.

Jake I'm sorry.

Giles I seem to be the only one who didn't know. You should have told me.

Jake I didn't know how to.

Giles I was very . . . I'm going to have to be very careful how I talk to her – we both are, Jake.

Jake Sure.

Giles She'll obviously be feeling terrible about it. Guilt, probably, and insecurity and rejection . . .

Jake Rejection?

Giles Well, I understand it was Teddy who broke it off . . .

Jake Yes, sure, but . . .

Giles All I'm saying is, Jake, your mother's a very special person and we'll have to nurse her back to emotional health. That's all. She needs us.

Jake What about you? Don't you feel a bit rejected, a bit hurt . . .?

Giles Well, yes. Naturally. But when something like this happens with someone like Jo . . . It's yourself you rather tend to question. What went wrong? What drove her to do it? Do you see?

Jake Well, I'd have thought it was fairly obvious what –

Giles She's complex. I met her, you know, when I was still a medical student . . .

Jake Yes, I know . . .

Giles She was a drama student at that time, you know. But she never went on with that, which was a pity, she could have been really good. I saw her once in one of her end of term shows, you know – but then she decided she wanted to teach instead – so – anyway, we met at this dance. She came with another student – she was – she was quite the most beautiful person in the room actually – and I started staring at her, you know – the way you do. You're not supposed to but you do. You don't expect anything to come of it, it's just I couldn't take my eyes off her – she was just so – incredibly beautiful. And she was dancing away with all these nine-foot-tall Adonises and I was thinking, oh well, home for cocoa – or whatever – and suddenly she was standing there at my table – looking down at me. And you can imagine, I jumped about a foot. And she said, are you going to ask me for a dance or are you just going to sit there staring all evening. And I said, sorry, I'm not an awfully good dancer actually. And she said, well, that's too bad because I'm going to have to spend the rest of the evening teaching you, aren't I? And I said, fair enough. That's fine by me. And then for the rest of the – rest of the – evening I danced with this . . . with this . . . with this . . . beautiful . . .

Giles is suddenly crying. Jake watches rather helplessly.

I'm sorry, Jake. I don't think I want to talk about this just at the moment if you don't mind . . .

Jake No, no. Fine . . .

Giles Poor you. The last thing you need is a crying father, isn't it? Got problems of your own, haven't you?

Jake Go right ahead.

Giles No, no. Sorry for myself, that's all. Pathetic. (*fiercely to himself*) Come on! Come on! Come on!

Barry and Lindy have re-entered.

Barry That's it, you tell him, Giles. That's telling him.

Giles What? Oh, yes . . . (*He smiles weakly.*)

Lindy You listen to your father, eh?

Barry Father knows best, eh?

They set down their latest load.

Right. On we go . . . By the way, if either of you are suddenly moved to lend a hand, we won't object. (*He laughs.*)

Giles I'm so sorry, I would normally. It's just I'm expected up at the house in a minute, otherwise . . .

Barry Alright for some, eh? It's a sandwich in the back of the Transit for us . . .

Jake You're going up to the house for lunch?

Lindy Think about the workers.

Giles Yes, Trish is expecting us.

Jake (*to Barry*) Sorry. I'm afraid I'm doing an interview.

Giles The last thing we should do is let her down.

Barry All offers gratefully received . . .

Barry and Lindy go off.

Giles I have to say, I'd prefer to be anywhere else but – sitting down at the same table as – I could do without this wretched fête this afternoon too, actually.

Jake Do you have to be here? Can't you – ?

Giles No, no. Not possibly. My whole troop's turning up. I couldn't let them down. They're relying on me.

Jake Your troop?

Giles Yes.

Jake You're going to be Morris dancing as well?

Giles Yes, of course. I know you think it's all very silly and quaint, Jake –

Jake No. It just seems sort of inappropriate today, that's all. How can you possibly Morris dance at a time like this?

Giles It's enormous fun. Great camaraderie. I wouldn't miss it for the world. I won't have my heart fully in it today of course, but . . . No, I couldn't possibly let them down. Anyway, take me out of myself, won't it? I must go and have a word with your mother. Collect her for lunch. I hope she's remembered . . . See you in a minute.

Jake Yes.

Giles We ought to talk more often.

Jake Yes.

Giles Any time you need a . . . I'm here for you, you know that, Jake.

Jake Thanks very much, Dad.

Giles gives him a thumbs up sign and goes off.
As he does so, Barry and Lindy return with more gear.

Barry . . . Right . . . ?

Lindy . . . right . . .

Barry . . . putting it down then . . .

Lindy . . . putting it down . . .

Both . . . Hooof!

They set this bundle down with the other things.

Lindy Whew! Just trying to remember. The fortune tent went there, didn't it? That I do remember.

Barry No. Over there. I've written it all down. I have the plan.

Lindy I'm sure it was over there.

Barry I have the plan!

A silent moment between them.

Don't let's argue and spoil the day, Lindy. Come along. Winnie awaits. Plenty more to unload.

Barry and Lindy go off. Sally returns from the house. She has changed out of her uniform.

Sally (*indicating her briefcase*) Oh, there it is. Thought I'd left it up at the school. Major panic over.

Jake I was going to bring it up to you . . .

Sally Thank God. Got my whole life in here . . . I saw you talking to your dad.

Jake Yes.

Sally How was he?

Jake Bit shaken up, really. He had such total trust in Mum, you see, it's come as a terrible shock. I don't think he can quite believe it. He keeps blaming himself.

Sally Himself? Why?

Jake God knows. Because he's – because he's my father. Who blames himself for everything. If it rains this afternoon, he'll blame himself for that. How's your mum?

Sally Well, not blaming herself, certainly. I don't think she's ever blamed herself for anything. She usually finds somebody else to blame. Me, for instance. My father, of course, is sailing on as usual as if it was nothing to do with him. Having long talks to the slightly sinister Gavin Ryng-Mayne. With a Y.

Jake Sinister?

Sally Yes, I find him a bit creepy. He was being awfully, awfully charming to me all the way up to the house. Which is always a bit suspicious with someone you've only just met. What's he doing here, I wonder?

Jake Come for lunch, hasn't he?

Sally Ha, ha. All the way from London? Not a chance. No, there's something brewing. He's not just a writer, he's quite politically involved, too. You know, personal adviser, writing speeches and so on . . .

Jake How do you know?

Sally I have my sources.

Jake (*smiling*) Really?

Sally (*smiling*) Yes.

Jake And you find him creepy?

Sally Well, that's not the right word. Just a bit underhand. A tiny bit – I don't know. Unscrupulous. Actually rather attractive.

Jake Oh, I see. Here we go . . .

Sally No, not in that way. For God's sake, he's my father's age. They were at school together. What do you think I am? You just sit there and wait for your elderly film star . . .

Jake She's not elderly . . .

Sally Aha . . . aha . . . Have you got your notebook?

Jake Yes. And my recorder. Which I hope she'll let me use.

Sally Cheat.

Jake No. I'll use both. Shorthand and a recorder. Most people do these days. Make doubly sure.

Sally What are you going to ask her?

Jake I don't know. How she likes this country . . .

Sally Boring!

Jake I've been told to ask that. Has she ever been to a garden fête before?

Sally Predictable!

Jake Did she enjoy working on a film in England?

Sally Does she find English men attractive?

Jake No. As it happens I'm not asking her that . . .
I'll talk about her working methods, whether they're
different, continental methods . . .

Sally Ask her what she's doing here.

Jake How do you mean?

Sally Well, why is she here?

Jake Well, she's publicising the film presumably.

Sally I beg your pardon. At a fête? At a garden *fête*? Big
budget movie, is it?

Jake See what you mean. I hadn't thought of that.

Sally Maybe she's having a secret affair.

Jake Who with?

Slight pause.

Both (*laughing*) Gavin Ryng-Mayne!

Jake With a Y.

Sally Do you think he has a brother with an X? Gavin
Rynx Manx?

They laugh.

Interview me, then.

Jake What?

Sally Come on. Interview me. Practice for you.

Jake Serious?

Sally Yes. Serious.

Jake (*producing his notebook and recorder*) Alright.
Hang about. Ready?

Sally (*preening herself*) Just a minute, yes.

Jake Serious. You've got to take it seriously.

Sally I will. Go on, then.

Jake Sally Platt, you come from a family with a long tradition of politicians – grandfather, great grandfather. Do you intend to follow in their footsteps?

Sally Well, it's a bit early for me to decide just at the moment. I am considering it.

Jake But you are excited by politics.

Sally Yes, I am. I've always been very practical, in that I've never enjoyed being just an onlooker. Ever since I was a child I've always wanted to be in control. I consider politics to be the most practical way to take control of my life.

Jake And presumably to some extent other people's?

Sally Possibly. To some extent.

Jake You think you're qualified to do that? To control the lives of others?

Sally You're making it sound as if I'd be standing as dictator. I'd merely be pursuing their best interests. Nothing to do with controlling them.

Jake Nonetheless, you feel you're the person to do it?

Sally Well, presumably if they'd elected me, they would too.

Jake What if I didn't vote for you? And I didn't feel your choices were in my best interests?

Sally Too bad. That's called democracy.

Jake OK. How about other interests? Do you have any hobbies?

Sally Well, I make a lot of jam. And I do embroidery at weekends . . .

Jake Come on! Come on!

Sally Well, honestly! Hobbies. I'm also waiting for the right man to come along, before you ask . . .

Jake Are you?

Sally What?

Jake Waiting for the right man?

Sally Certainly not.

Jake Truthfully?

Sally Not at the moment. I'm too busy with A-levels, anyway.

Jake By that, I take it you're not in love with anyone at the moment?

Sally (*uneasy now*) No. None of your business, anyway.

Jake But you do have feelings for people?

Sally Of course I do. What is this?

Jake Feelings you prefer to hide? Keep hidden? Because perhaps they frighten you? Maybe you're a bit afraid of them? Strong emotions?

Sally I'm stopping this now, this is getting stupid.

Jake Sometimes you write them down, don't you?

Sally (*flippantly*) Yes, in my diary. Every night. How did you guess?

Jake I was thinking more about poetry.

   A silence.

Sally (*quietly*) What?

Jake I said, you write poetry.

Sally (*taking this in*) Have you been in my briefcase? You've been in my bloody briefcase, haven't you?

Jake Just this one poem. It fell out, I couldn't help –

Sally No, it didn't. It didn't fall out at all. You rifled through my briefcase and you read it. How dare you? You bastard!

Jake Look, all I did was –

Sally (*livid*) How dare you go through my private belongings! How dare you!

Jake Listen, Sally, I didn't . . .

Sally (*grabbing up her case and leaving*) Well, that's it. That's it, as far as I'm concerned! Don't ever speak to me again!

Jake Sally . . .

Sally Fuck you!

Sally goes off. Jake sits appalled.

Jake (*in despair*) Oh, my God! What have I done? What have I done?

Joanna and Giles have entered in time to hear this last. They are walking in silence, well apart from each other. Joanna now crosses to Jake and hugs him to her, somewhat melodramatically.

Joanna (*in a low voice*) Jake, my darling. You mustn't blame yourself. It's all us. It's not your fault. It's all us.

She releases him and starts again, walking towards the house. As he passes, Giles pats Jake affectionately on the shoulder.
Joanna and Giles go off. Jake continues to sit miserably on the grass.
Barry and Lindy return with yet more stuff.

Barry . . . OK . . .?

Lindy . . . OK . . .

Barry . . . nearly the lot . . .

Lindy . . . nearly the lot . . .

Barry . . . one – two . . . huuup!

Lindy (*with him*) . . . Huuup!

They set this down with the rest.

Barry Whew!

Lindy Whew!

Barry (*to Jake*) We've got Winnie loaded to the gunwales, today . . .

Jake Oh, yes.

Lindy That's our van. The Transit. We call her Winnie.

Warn enters, looking particularly out of sorts.
Jake, under the next, wanders away down one of the paths.

Warn Two rear wheels on the verge back there . . .

Lindy Oh, dear . . .

Barry Now who was supposed to be seeing me back? Make sure that precise thing didn't happen? Whose job was that?

Lindy Sorry.

Barry Don't apologise to me. It's Warn you should be apologising to.

Lindy Sorry.

Barry Sorry, Warn, I'm afraid we have my wife to blame for that . . .

Lindy So sorry.

Barry (*hurrying off*) Don't worry, Warn, I'll move her straight away. Don't worry, Lindy, stay there. I'll see myself forward, it'll be safer. (*Barry goes off.*)

Warn (*muttering*) Too late now. Buggered, in' they?

Lindy (*after Barry, vainly*) Shall I start unpacking some of this . . .? (*to Warn*) So, so, sorry.

> Lindy starts to unpack the upright poles that will form the enclosure.
> Izzie enters from the house. She has a sandwich box with Warn's lunch.

Izzie Here, your lunch, then. You're lucky to get it at all. It's chaos up there. Total hymen. All arriving at the wrong time through the wrong gates. Why'd you move all the signs today, then, eh?

> Warn does not reply

God, you're a cantabulous old bastard, aren't you? (*She pauses for breath.*) Well, I don't know. The carrots are par-boiled, the beans are waitin', my puddin's are poised, the roast potatoes are shot and that beef's been in and out so many times, it's like a candle in a spinster's bedroom. I'm not answerable. I told her, I can't be answerable. She should have had pork. You can muck about with pork; you can't do that with beef.

> Warn watches Lindy impassively.

Well . . . (*seeing something in the direction of the house*) Oh, no. Is that them? Yes, there's a car. Must be them. I'd better get back. You behave yourself this afternoon, that's all. I'll be watching both of you.

> Izzie hurries off to the house.
> Jake comes on.

163

Jake Did someone say a car?

Lindy I think there's one just arrived, Jake . . .

Jake At last. (*Jake hurries off after Izzie.*)

Lindy Oh! Great excitement, isn't there?

> *Warn does not deign to reply.*
> *Barry comes back with a few more items.*

Barry Car just arriving . . .

Lindy Yes, we know. That'll be her, I expect.

Barry It seems to be heading round the back there. Like the other one.

Lindy Oh . . .

Barry No signs, are there?

> *Warn goes off.*

I think I'd better serve as welcoming committee again, hadn't I?

Lindy I'll come with you.

Barry No, Lindy. You carry on with that. That's more important. I can do it.

> *Fran, Lucille's driver, appears down the path. She seems fairly formidable.*

Fran (*in a flat London voice*) Excuse me. Do you know how we get to the house from here?

Barry Ah, good morning. Are you Madame Cadeau? Lucille Cadeau?

Fran No, I'm not. I'm the driver.

Barry Oh, right. Sorry for the confusion. Barry Love, how do you do?

Lindy (*unnoticed*) Hallo.

Barry Now then. You can either get in your car, make a U-turn, return down the back drive and once you come to the fork, take the right one not the left one, otherwise you'll finish up at the home farm, over the cattle grid and then, when you get to the bottom, you're on the road again. Turn right, it's a bit of a blind corner so be careful, up to the cross-roads, very much the way you came, then right again – don't go straight on because that just takes you the back way to the village –

Lindy Past our house . . .

Barry Yes, thank you, Lindy, I don't think that's particularly relevant – right at the cross-roads and then go very slowly up the hill till you'll see on your right, clearly signposted – well, it isn't clearly signposted at present because it's been temporarily removed – normally clearly signposted a notice to the house. And you take that right and you'll find yourself at the front door. Is that clear enough?

Fran (*dryly*) Beautiful.

Barry Want me to repeat it for you?

Fran No, thank you.

Barry Or else you can walk straight up that path there. Probably be quicker.

> *At this moment, Lucille appears along one of the paths. She is everything expected of a French film star, attractive, vivacious and charming.*

* **Lucille** Que c'est beau ici . . .

Barry Ah! Here she is!

Lindy Hallo. This must be her.

---

* It's so beautiful here . . .

* **Lucille** C'est sublime non! Je n'aurais jamais imaginé que ce serait aussi beau.

Barry (*moving forward to greet her*) How do you do? Lucille? I'm Barry. Welcome. May I call you Lucille?

Lucille Hallo. (*to Fran*) C'est le propriétaire, c'est Monsieur Plate?

Lindy (*unnoticed*) Hallo.

Fran Non, je ne sais pas qui c'est, l'idiot du village, je crois . . .

Barry How – finding – you – our – countryside?

Fran Nous sommes arrivées par la porte arrière, parait-il.

Lucille Il y avait aucun panneau.

Fran Quelqu'un les a arrachés. Cet idiot peut-être. Ce serait sans doute plus rapide d'y aller à pied. Ça ne vous ennuie pas de marcher?

Lucille Non. Après quatre heures enfermée dans cette voiture . . .

---

* **Lucille** Isn't this the most glorious place? I had no idea it was going to be this beautiful.

Barry (*moving forward to greet her*) How do you do? Lucille? I'm Barry. Welcome. May I call you Lucille?

Lucille Hallo. (*to Fran*) Is this the owner, is this Mr Plate?

Lindy (*unnoticed*) Hallo.

Fran No, I don't know who he is, the local village idiot, I think . . .

Barry How – finding – you – our – countryside?

Fran We've come to the back gate, apparently.

Lucille There weren't any signposts.

Fran Somebody's pulled them all up. Perhaps this lunatic. It's maybe quicker to walk. Do you mind walking?

Lucille No. After four hours in that car . . .

166

Barry Have – you – much – been – out – of – London – before?

Fran We'll walk. It's OK.

Barry Oh, yes. Permit me to show you . . .

Fran (*sharply*) It's alright, honestly. Thanks very much.

Barry Well . . .

* **Fran** Vite, on ne va jamais se débarrasser de lui. La maison est par ici.

Lucille (*as they go*) Quel petit bonhomme extraordinaire. Ils sont tous comme ça par ici?

Fran Très probablement. Je vous l'ai dit, nous avons abandonné la civilisation après Hammersmith . . .

Lucille and Fran go off towards the house.

Barry Well. What a beautiful woman. Absolutely stunning, wasn't she? Took your breath away.

Lindy You might have introduced me.

Barry Now that's what I call an attractive woman. Only the French, eh? Only the French. Frenchwomen, they have that – je ne sais quoi – that little extra, don't they?

Lindy Another leg, you mean?

Barry (*unamused*) Don't be silly, Lindy. Don't be silly now.

Jake enters breathlessly from one of the paths.

Jake Where've they gone?

---

* **Fran** Quick, we'll never get rid of him. The house is this way.

Lucille (*as they go*) What an extraordinary little man. Are they all like that round here?

Fran Very likely. I told you, we left civilisation after Hammersmith . . .

Barry Sorry?

Jake I got to the front gate, they drove right past. I've just chased them round to the back gate.

Lindy They're walking up to the house.

Jake Oh, grief . . . (*Jake runs off after them.*)

Barry He's not going to catch them, is he? Never make a paparazzi.

Lindy Poor boy. I feel so sorry for him.

Barry Jake? Let's get started on these poles, shall we? Why should you feel sorry for Jake?

They start to sort out the poles that Lindy has unpacked, during the next.

Lindy Well . . . all this business with his parents.

Barry Oh, you mean the carryings on?

Lindy Shh! Yes. Can't be nice for him, can it?

Barry Don't imagine it would be. I think we've got time to lay these out you know, Lindy. Then we'll sit in Winnie and have an early sandwich and wait for the rest of the mob. Now, let's see . . .

Lindy Do you think that could ever happen to us?

Barry What?

Lindy You know. One of us going off with someone?

Barry Certainly not. What are you saying?

Lindy Don't you ever think about it?

Barry No.

Lindy Not even now and then?

Barry I've got better things to do with my time, Lindy. And so have you. Now hold that. (*He hands her a pole.*)

Lindy I think about it now and then.

Barry What? Us having love affairs?

Lindy Well, you having love affairs, mostly.

Barry Me? That's not very likely, I must say.

Lindy Why not?

Barry Because I've got you, haven't I? More than a handful.

Lindy Don't you ever get bored with me?

Barry You're exciting enough for me, Lindy.

Lindy I get bored with me. Sometimes I get so bored with me. I don't know how you stand it sometimes. I wouldn't. If I were you, I'd go off. I would.

Barry (*sitting on the grass*) Sit down for a moment, Lindy.

Lindy sits beside him.

You see that yellow car out there, Lindy? The one that man was driving? That's a Porsche, Lindy.

Lindy I know. Beautiful.

Barry Now. Could you ever in a million years, even given all the lottery money we could spend, could you ever imagine me behind the wheel of that?

Lindy No, not really.

Barry Conversely, could you ever imagine yourself behind the wheel of that?

Lindy I can't even drive . . .

Barry Now, what's parked next to that vehicle, next to the Porsche?

Lindy Our old Transit.

Barry Exactly. Good old faithful Winnie. Winnie, the Transit. And how do we both feel about Winnie?

Lindy We're very fond of her.

Barry (*patting her leg*) What more can I say than that? (*He bounds up.*) Now hold that pole upright for a minute and I'll walk back a bit and line it up, alright? Just hold it there.

> *Barry goes off along the path. Lindy stands unhappily, holding the pole.*
> *Jake returns from the house, even more out of breath. He flops on the grass.*

Jake Missed them! After all that.

Lindy (*in her own thoughts*) Oh, dear.

Barry (*off, distant*) That's it, Lindy. Keep it upright! Keep it upright!

Jake What are you doing?

Lindy Holding this pole.

Jake Oh, yes. Have you seen that car out there? The Porsche. Beautiful. I wouldn't mind driving that.

Lindy What about the one next to it?

Jake What, the old bashed up Transit, you mean?

Lindy That's ours.

Jake Oh, no offence.

Lindy Fancy driving that, do you?

Jake Well, frankly, not a lot, no.

Lindy No, I didn't think you would somehow.

Lindy suddenly throws down the pole and hurries off, weeping. Jake is rather startled.

Jake (*puzzled*) Sorry? (*to himself*) What did I say?

Barry (*off, distant*) Lindy! Don't let go of it! Lindy? What are you doing? Lindy?

Warn comes on with his sandwiches. He sits and starts to eat. Jake lies out.

Jake I don't think this is my day somehow.

A distant rumble of thunder.

Warn (*looking at the sky, with satisfaction*) Here it comes.

He continues to sit there as the lights fade to:
Blackout.

Act Two

SCENE ONE

Saturday, August 14th, 2.00 p.m.
The same.
*It is overcast and, to everyone but the most optimistic,
clearly about to rain.*
*Some things have been set up including the Maypole.
Several of the stalls, including the hoop-la, are also
complete.*
*Jake comes on anxiously as though looking for
someone. There are sounds of activity all around and
occasionally people come in and out of sight.*

Jake (*calling vaguely in all directions*) Mum . . . Mum!

Barry passes busily.

Barry (*unconcerned*) No sign of her?

Jake No . . .

Barry She'll turn up. (*as he goes*) She's got her Maypole
dance, hasn't she? She won't miss that. We'll be opening
the gates in just a minute . . . (*Barry goes.*)

Jake (*calling*) Mum . . .

The bushes rustle and Joanna's voice is heard.

Joanna (*hissing*) Jake . . . Jake . . . Jake . . .

Jake (*trying to locate her*) Mum?

Joanna Jake . . .

Jake Where are you?

Joanna Over here. In the bushes . . .

Jake (*seeing her*) Oh, there you are. What are you –

Joanna (*fiercely*) No! Don't look in my direction!

Jake What?

Joanna You mustn't give away my position, whatever you do. He mustn't know I'm here. It's vital he doesn't know I'm here . . .

Jake Who? Who mustn't know? Who are we talking about, Mum?

Joanna Ssssh! Keep your voice down . . .

Jake Sorry. Mum, I don't know what's going on. Why are you in the bushes?

Joanna I'm hiding from him.

Jake Him?

Joanna Harold.

Jake Harold?

Joanna Jake, I have something terrible to tell you.

Jake Who's Harold?

Joanna You have to know. You have a right to know. You're my son, you have a right to know these things . . .

Jake Mum, I wish you'd come out of the bushes, it's very hard trying to talk to you –

Joanna I'm trying to tell you, Jake, it's –

Barry and Lindy come on carrying more stuff.

Shhh! Later! Walk away! Walk away! You haven't seen me. Please!

Jake walks away.

Jake My God, what's happening?

Lindy Alright, Jake?

Jake Yes, yes. Sure. I just need to find my dad. (*Jake goes off towards the house somewhat dazed.*)

Barry (*laughing*) Lost his dad as well. This is unforgivable, you know. There should be thirty volunteer helpers here. And how many are there? Four. Including you and me. And old Mr Eldridge whose foot's so bad he can't lift anything anyway. We're way behind. Way behind.

Lindy I know, dear, you keep saying . . .

Barry We've never been so behind. In eleven years of organising this – even during the floods – we were never this far behind . . . Have you checked the tent? Lindy?

Lindy (*who has become aware of Joanna in the bushes*) What?

Barry Do listen, Lindy, for heaven's sake . . . I said have you checked the tent?

Lindy Yes, I've already said. I put it up personally and checked it . . .

Barry That tent is your responsibility, you know . . .

Lindy (*distracted by something*) Yes . . . yes . . .

Barry I deliberately delegated that to you – What are you doing?

Lindy There's someone – (*confidentially*) . . . I think there's someone in the bushes over there . . .

Barry The bushes?

Lindy I saw the branches move.

Barry Are you sure?

Lindy Yes. There! Can you see?

Barry Good gracious!

Lindy Who is it?

Barry I've no idea.

Lindy It could be a lurker.

Barry I don't like the look of that. In another five minutes this place will be swarming with old people and youngsters . . .

Lindy It will. Toddlers.

Barry Just keep talking a minute . . .

Lindy What about?

Barry What does it matter? Just keep talking. I'm going to try and take them by surprise . . . Keep talking, go on.

Lindy (*after a second's thought*) I can't think of anything to say . . .

Barry Lindy, for goodness sake . . .!

As Lindy starts her recitation, Barry gives her a despairing look, then wanders casually close to the bushes to investigate.

Lindy
We've got a nasty ickle baby come to live with us,
I fink it really isn't fair, the way they make a fuss
About a fing that's got no sense and hardly any hair,
And isn't half so pretty as my ickle Teddy Bear.
What is the use of baby? Well, I cannot really –

Barry pounces into the bushes with a cry. There is a great deal of commotion.

Barry Haaaarrrrrr!! (*He emerges.*)

Lindy You alright, dear . . .?

Barry They – ran off.

Lindy Did you see who it was?

Barry Yes. It was Joanna Mace. Mrs Mace.

Lindy Oh.

Barry She looked – quite wild. I would almost say dishevelled.

Lindy She's usually very smart.

Barry Exactly. Something wrong. Something very, very wrong. What was I saying earlier, Lindy? Precisely that. You indulge in extra-marital activities and look where you end up.

Lindy In the bushes.

Barry My point precisely. We'll have to keep an eye on her, she looked a trifle unbalanced. Certainly casts a shadow over the Maypole dance, doesn't it?

Lindy Oh, we can't cancel that!

Barry I hope it won't come to that.

Lindy They'd be so disappointed. They've all got their little costumes specially made and everything . . . We couldn't cancel it. It would break their hearts after all their rehearsing . . .

Barry I can assure you that will be a last resort. Since the dog handler's cancelled, I was relying on it as the high spot of the afternoon.

Warn and Izzie enter with some books for the stall.

(*to them*) Well done, well done. I think we're nearly there. Come on, Lindy. Follow me . . .

Giles comes on. He is dressed in his Morris dancer's outfit. He is also looking for Joanna.

Lindy (*seeing him, excitedly*) Oh, Giles . . . We've just seen Jo –

Barry (*quietening her, sharply*) Alright, Lindy! That'll do! That'll do!

Lindy What?

Barry Not in front of the world, if you don't mind. Discretion please.

Lindy Oh.

Giles What's going on?

Barry Off you go, Lindy. I'm sure you've got plenty to be getting on with . . .

Lindy Yes. I must be – getting on . . . Excuse me. (*to Giles*) I'm so sorry.

Lindy goes off.

Giles What's going on?

Barry I just wanted a quiet word if I could.

Giles Really?

Barry Man to man. In your ear.

Under the next, Warn and Izzie go off again.

Giles Look, if it's about John Whittle I'm sorry. I'm sorry, I have tried his mobile but I'm not getting any reply. He's certainly left home anyway, I ascertained that.

Barry Pardon?

Giles John Whittle, our Morris dance co-ordinator. I don't know where on earth they can all be. I hope nothing's happened to them.

Barry I'm sure they'll turn up, I'm sure they will. Listen, Giles, this is a bit embarrassing, a bit awkward but – frankly – the wife.

Giles Lindy? Is something wrong? She does look a little –

Barry No, no, not Lindy, I'm not talking about Lindy. Joanna.

Giles Ah.

Barry Nothing the matter with Lindy. Lindy's perfectly fine. It's all in her head. No, Joanna. Look, Giles, I have no wish to pry into your private affairs. As we know full well, women, bless them, are creatures of whim . . .

Giles That's perfectly alright, Barry. None of my affairs are any longer private. Feel free to discuss them along with the rest of the village . . .

Barry I'm sorry, it must be very –

Giles (*quite sharply, for him*) Yes, it is, actually. If you want to know. It is. Very. Now, what is it you want to tell me?

Barry (*secretively*) The bottom line. She's in the bushes. She's been sighted. Lurking in the bushes.

Giles What's she doing in the bushes?

Barry I rather hoped you could tell me.

Giles I've no idea. She rushed away in the middle of lunch. Threw down her cutlery and fled –

Barry Don't get me wrong. It's a free country. I'm as broad-minded as the next man. I'm just a little worried she might alarm people. Once we let the general public in. I was thinking particularly of old folk, you know, they can get a trifle apprehensive if they feel they're being observed from the shrubbery . . .

Giles Well, alright, I'll see if I can – I can locate her. Where's Jake, I wonder? I rather need Jake.

Barry (*starting up towards the house*) He was here a minute ago. He may have gone up to the house, looking for you. I'll tell you what I'll do. When I come back, I'll get Lindy to muster the little Maypole dancers. If we can group them round their pole, that might just serve to lure Joanna out of hiding.

Giles (*doubtfully*) Yes, I suppose that's possible.

Barry I'm just popping up to the house, to inform the official party we're ready to start. (*loudly*) Everyone to your posts, please. We'll be opening the gates in a few minutes.

Barry goes off towards the house.
   Giles, somewhat aimlessly, starts to look into the shrubbery in the hope of locating Joanna.
   Warn and Izzie enter with some more books.

Izzie I been made a mockery today. I been held up and humidified. I never cooked a meal like it. Never. There were this Frenchwoman there. Expecting her Gordon Blue. And what's she get? Had to throw the rest of that beef away. Spoof wouldn't touch it neither.

They set down their load.

I left her washing up. Little madam. Kitchen'll be full of debrage when I get back. She wants electrocuting and hanging up by her hair, that girl. Pouring wine with half her chest hanging out. That doctor, he was practically down inside her vest. I don't care what you say, she needs a dad. She needs a man's firm hand, Warn.

Warn clears his throat in a sort of growl.

And I don't want to hear no more arguments, neither. She were always too young for you, even when you were younger, she were still too young for you but that were alright then, what you two did in your own home were your own business. But now I'm moved in that's all changed. Because she's my daughter and now you're sleepin' with me that makes you her father whether you like it or not. And it ain't right to sleep with your own daughter. Because now you're committin' incense and that's a seven deadly sin, I know that 'cause it's in the Bible, right?

Warn moves off.

(*calling*) You can walk away. Don't make no difference.

Warn is about to exit in the direction of the house but he nearly collides with Pearl. She is now dressed in her fortune-telling outfit.

Warn (*moving away*) Bloody women.

Warn goes off.

Pearl What you done to him?

Izzie You behave like a daughter, you hear? Or you'll feel my wrath. (*Izzie goes off.*)

Pearl (*despairingly, to herself*) How can I behave like a daughter when he don't even want to be a father? He don't want a daughter. He don't want me as a daughter. He only wanted me for lust. That's all he wanted me for. What's he want a daughter for? (*glaring after Izzie*) This'd never have happened if you hadn't pinched him off me in the first place.

Giles emerges from the bushes. Pearl watches him.

Giles Oh, I give up ... I really do ... (*calling*) Joanna ...! Jo!

He sees Pearl. She smiles at him.

Pearl Still looking for her, then?

Giles Er, yes ... Just ...

Pearl What makes you think she'll be in the bushes, then?

Giles Er – just a – wild hunch.

Pearl No reason for her to be in the bushes, is there?

Giles Probably not.

Pearl (*significantly*) Not today, anyway.

Giles droops a little.

(*instantly regretting this*) Sorry. No call for that. Sorry.

Pause.

Shame you had to rush away from your dinner, though.

Giles Yes. As I explained, my wife suddenly remembered she had a very important phone call from overseas that she simply had to take. And then I remembered that stupidly I'd not given her the number. In case they wanted her to call them back.

Pearl Missed your treacle tart, didn't you? (*twirling for his approval*) Like my new fortune-telling dress?

Giles Very nice.

Pearl Coming in my tent this year, are you? Have your fortune told?

Giles Well, I don't – I don't – I don't think so. I already have a fairly clear idea of my fortune. I don't think I want to know much more about it.

Pearl Fortunes can change.

Giles Sometimes.

Pearl (*smiling at him again*) Be surprised.

Giles I think at your age that's possible, Pearl. But at my age . . .

Jake appears from the house during the next.

Pearl Your age? Get on with you. I'm acquainted with older men than you, I can tell you. Prefer a bit of vintage, me.

Giles Yes, I . . . did realise. Well, I'm certainly vintage. Practically oxidised, I'm afraid. (*He laughs a little.*)

Pearl (*shrugging*) I'm into most things. Try anything once . . .

Giles (*seeing Jake*) Ah, Jake.

Jake (*a little mystified by what he's overheard*) Hallo.

Pearl Oh. Best get my camera. Nearly forgot. Always nice to get a photo, isn't it? See you later.

Pearl smiles at them both and goes off.
Giles and Jake stand awkwardly, each not knowing quite where to start.

Jake Just been – up to the house.

Giles Oh, yes.

Jake Thought you might be up there.

Giles No, I'm – I'm down here.

Jake Yes.

A pause.

Giles Listen, there's no easy way to do this – I'm going to have to plunge straight in. Apparently, Joanna, your mother is – is – is –

Jake In the – in the – bushes.

Giles – bushes. Yes, you knew?

Jake Yes. As a matter of fact, I spoke to her.

182

Giles You did?

Jake Yes.

Giles How was she?

Jake A bit – strange. The point is, I think I've got some really bad news for you.

Giles Go on.

Jake Well, you know all along we were thinking – well, most of us were thinking that she was just having an affair with Mr Platt. I've got a feeling there was someone else as well.

Giles Someone else? Who? Tell me?

Jake Er – it's er – it's er – Harold.

Giles Harold?

Jake That's what she said.

Giles Who is Harold?

Jake That's what I asked her.

Giles And she said?

Jake She – said she'd tell me later. She wanted to talk to me on my own. She seems to think people are after her. That's why she's hiding.

Giles Yes, yes. Well, I suppose you'd better try to do that. I'll leave you to it. It's obvious she doesn't want me, isn't it? Harold . . .

Jake Dad, I don't think Mum knows at the moment what she wants. I wouldn't take it too personally.

Giles It's bloody hard not to, Jake, it really is. Harold . . . OK, I'll keep out of the way. I'll be over there by the Bat the Rat. Call me if you think I can be of any help.

Jake Right. Assuming I can find her.

Giles I think she's nearby. I – have a feeling she's watching us, don't you?

Jake Yes.

Giles I'll tell Lindy to round up the Maypole dancers. Barry has this theory that if we group them round their pole it might lure Joanna out.

Jake Sort of Judas goat, you mean?

Giles (*smiling weakly*) That sort of thing, yes. (*a wave of depression sweeping over him*) Harold . . . God, what sort of husband, am I? Married to a serial adulteress and I didn't even realise. God . . .

> *Giles leaves. Jake, on his own, moves round the garden, calling gently to various clumps of bushes. Two very small bandsmen pass clutching oversized brass instruments.*

Jake Mum . . . Mum . . . are you in there? Mum . . .

Joanna (*from within a clump of bushes*) Jake?

Jake Yes, it's me.

Joanna Has he gone?

Jake Dad? Yes, he's gone.

Joanna No, Harold. Has Harold gone, Jake?

Jake Mum, I don't really know any Harold – nor does Dad. Do you think you'd like to come out of the bushes now? It's perfectly safe.

Joanna I can't come out, Jake. If Harold catches sight of me talking to you, that'll put you in terrible danger as well . . .

Jake It will?

Joanna You don't know him, Jake. Nobody spotted him. He's been so clever. He's had us all fooled. He's been so diabolically clever . . .

Jake Who has?

Joanna Harold!

Joanna emerges slightly from the bushes in order to draw Jake closer to her. Her clothes are torn and she is covered in leaves and twigs.

Jake, listen very carefully . . .

Jake (*alarmed at her appearance*) Mum . . .

Joanna Listen! Listen! I haven't much time. He may catch up with me at any minute. That man is not your father.

Jake Who's not my father?

Joanna That man you were talking to just now. He is not your father.

Jake Do you mean Dad?

Joanna Yes ! Yes!

Jake Dad's not my father?

Joanna No! No! Why are you being so stupid all of a sudden, Jake?

Jake I don't – I don't – I don't – I don't – I don't – know – I . . .

Joanna You're never normally stupid. He's not your father, Jake. He has never been your father. Can you get that through your head?

Jake I see. I see. Let's get this straight. Somebody else is my father, then?

Joanna Yes.

Jake But not that man?

Joanna No.

Jake Then who's my father, Mum?

Joanna Giles. Giles is your real father.

Jake But that was Giles, Mum. The man I was just talking to. That was Giles.

Joanna No, no, it wasn't, it wasn't!

Jake Then who was that?

Joanna That was Harold. They replaced Giles. They replaced your father with Harold.

Jake Who? Who's replaced my father with Harold?

Joanna I don't know, do I? They're doing these things all the time. And the terrifying thing is that I never realised. Harold's been in our home for years. All the time you were growing up, Jake. And I never even realised.

Jake Mum, what makes you think that man isn't Giles?

Joanna Because if you'd known the real Giles you'd have seen through this man, Jake. Like I should have done years ago. God, I've been so blind. Giles, the real Giles was the gentlest man in the world, Jake. He loved me so much. He used to hold me in the night, you know . . . when I needed him. He gave me so much love. I would never have had to go to anybody else for love if Giles had still been here, Jake. You must believe that. I would never have done something like that. Giles was all I ever needed. He was so tender, so understanding. I wish you'd known him, Jake. I would never have hurt the real Giles like this . . .

Jake And this man – Harold – he doesn't do any of that . . .?

Joanna (*with a shudder*) Harold? Harold doesn't love me. Harold doesn't love anybody. Jake, he's not even human. He's like a machine. A cold, heartless machine. He doesn't love me, he doesn't love you.

Jake Why do you call him Harold?

Joanna Because I finally caught him out, Jake. We were walking up to the house this morning and I called out, Harold! And he turned round, Jake, he turned round and looked straight at me. And I thought, gotcha! He wouldn't have done that if his name wasn't Harold, would he?

Jake Listen, why don't you come with me and we'll find – Harold – and perhaps, you know, we can discuss this. Just the three of us.

Joanna (*drawing back*) With Harold? You want us to talk with Harold? What are you suggesting? He's got at you too, hasn't he? He's got at you? Oh, God, are you Jake? Maybe you're not even Jake . . .

Jake Mum . . .

Joanna (*drawing back deeper into the bushes*) Get away! Get away from me! You're not my son! My son would have understood! Jake would have understood!

Jake Oh, God . . .

  He stands, uncertainly, then waves to his father. Giles comes hurrying on.

Giles Well . . .

Jake It's rather complicated, Dad. I don't know quite where to start.

Joanna (*from the bushes, calling*) Gordon!

Jake (*turning, startled*) What?

Joanna (*triumphantly*) Gotcha!

Giles Jake, what on earth is –

He is interrupted by the arrival of Teddy and Lucille, both of whom have had rather a lot to drink. They enter from the direction of the house. They are accompanied by Barry. Lindy also returns from another direction, having assembled Joanna's young Maypole dancers. Also Warn and Izzie.

* **Lucille** (*as they enter*) . . . c'est absolument magnifique. J'adore vos merveilleux jardins, ils sont si sauvages, si authentiques . . .

Teddy (*not understanding a word*) All of that, yes. As far as the eye can see. Right, here we are everyone . . .

Lindy (*over this*) Right, Maypole dancers into your starting positions, please. (*to Barry*) We've opened the gates.

Barry Were there many waiting?

Lindy About eight.

Barry Ah, well. They'll come later. They often come along later.

Barry goes off. Teddy and Lucille make a tour of inspection. Lindy gathers the dancers.

† **Lucille** (*examining the hoop-la*) C'est quoi ça? Ça?

Teddy That? That's hoop-la. (*demonstrating*) You know, le hoop-la.

---

* . . . this is absolutely magnificent. I love your wonderful gardens, they're so wild and unspoiled . . .

† What is this? This?

* **Lucille** Ah, oui. Les anneaux. Je vois.

Jake (*moving in on them*) Excuse me, I'm from the press.

Lucille Pardon?

Teddy (*shouting*) He's from the press. A journalist.

Lucille Oh, c'est un journaliste.

Jake Excusez-moi. Mon français n'est pas très bon mais j'aimerais vous poser quelques questions.

Lucille (*amused*) Yes. We speak.

Jake Merci. D'abord. Est-ce-que c'est votre première visite dans cette région?

Lucille Oui, c'est ma premiére visite.

Jake Qu'est-ce-que vous en pensez?

Lucille Je trouve que c'est magnifique.

Jake Et qu'est-ce qui vous amène ici? Vous faites de la publicité pour le film? Vous êtes en vacances?

---

* **Lucille** Oh, yes. Hoop-la. I know it.

Jake (*moving in on them*) Excuse me, I'm from the press.

Lucille Sorry?

Teddy (*shouting*) He's from the press. A journalist.

Lucille Oh, he's a journalist.

Jake Excuse me. My French is not very good but I would like to ask you a few questions.

Lucille (*amused*) Yes. We speak.

Jake Thank you. Firstly. Is this the first time you have been to this part of our country?

Lucille Yes, this is the first time.

Jake How do you like it?

Lucille I find it very beautiful.

Jake And what brings you here? Are you promoting the film? Or on holiday?

* Lucille Non, je me rends dans une clinique.

Jake A clinic? Vous allez en clinique?

Lucille Oui. Pour ma santé.

Jake Oh, I see. You mean a health farm. Ici, on appelle ça un centre de remise en forme.

Lucille Non, non, non. Pas un centre de remise en forme. Je connais ça. Je parle d'une clinique. Pour une thérapie.

Jake Thérapie? Quelle sorte de thérapie?

Lucille Pour accoutumance, vous voyez.

Jake Addiction? Vous voulez dire la drogue?

Lucille La drogue aussi, mais seulment un peu. Surtout pour l'alcohol.

Fran has entered from the house.

Jake Alcohol . . . Je vois.

---

* **Lucille** No. I am on my way to a clinic.

Jake A clinic? You're on your way to a clinic?

Lucille Yes. For my health.

Jake Oh, I see. You mean a health farm. Over here we call them health farms.

Lucille No, no, no. Not a health farm. I know about health farms. This is a clinic. For therapy.

Jake Therapy? What sort of therapy?

Lucille For addiction, you know.

Jake Addiction? You mean drugs?

Lucille Drugs as well, but only a little. Mainly for alcohol.

Fran has entered from the house.

Jake Alcohol . . . I see.

* Fran Right. That's it. End of interview. Thank you. (*to Lucille*) Ne dites pas un mot de plus. Cet homme est journaliste, nom d'un chien . . .

Lucille shrugs and moves away rather sulkily.

Fran (*to Jake*) Forget anything she said, alright? That was off the record.

Jake I don't think it was, you know. It was very much on the record.

Fran You print one word of that, sunshine, we'll sue you, alright?

Jake Oh, yes? Who's we?

Fran Her agents, IMI. International Murder Incorporated.

Barry has returned with a hand mic.

Barry (*into mic*) Ladies and gentlemen. Thank you, everyone, who's braved –

He is interrupted by an eccentric fanfare from the offstage band. He pauses.

Our junior band, ladies and gentlemen, who this year are gallantly standing in for our senior band who have an unexpected prior engagement. As I was saying, thank you, everybody, who has braved the elements to come here today. Without fur –

An enormous clap of thunder and a torrential down pour. Everyone rushes for cover, pulling sheets of polythene over the uncovered stalls as they go. Barry, Lindy, Fran, Izzie and the children all head for the house. Teddy and Lucille dive into the tent. The garden is empty for a second or two. Then Lucille's head sticks out of the tent.

---

* Right. That's it. End of interview. Thank you. (*to Lucille*) Don't say another word. This man's a journalist, for God's sake . . .

* **Lucille** Quel déluge! Je n'ai jamais vu une pluie pareille. Il pleut toujours comme ça en Angleterre?

Teddy (*his head also appearing*) It's only a shower, I think. Probably all pass over in a – in a year or two . . .

Lucille Les pauvres. Et leur fête champêtre? Tout ce travail. C'est comme ça tous les ans?

> *The band strikes up again, playing a selection of discordant melodies.*

Teddy What the hell is that?

† **Lucille** (*coming out of the tent*) Oh, un orchestre! Avec de tous petits musiciens. Ce sont des nains?

Teddy Be careful! You'll get very wet. You – will – get – wet . . .

Lucille (*shrugging*) Oh, ce n'est pas grave. Mais, ce sont des enfants qui jouent. Des petits enfants, c'est mignon. Les instruments sont plus grands qu'eux. C'est adorable!

Teddy Bloody awful row. Where's the proper band, for God's sake?

> *Lucille wanders further away.*

---

* **Lucille** What a downpour! I've never seen rain like this. Does it always rain like this in England?

Teddy (*his head also appearing*) It's only a shower, I think. Probably all pass over in a – in a year or two . . .

Lucille Poor people. What about their garden fete? All this hard work. Is it like this every year?

† **Lucille** (*coming out of the tent*) Oh, look. It's a band. A band with very tiny players. Are they midgets?

Teddy Be careful! You'll get very wet. You – will – get – wet . . .

Lucille (*shrugging*) Oh, that's not important. Look, they're children playing. Little children, it's so sweet. The instruments are bigger than they are. It's enchanting!

(*still in the tent*) Lucille, what are you doing?

* **Lucille** Oh! Les anneaux! Je veux jouer aux anneaux!

Teddy Oh, for God's sake! You mad French person. (*coming out of the tent at last*) You want to play hoop-la, do you?

Lucille Oui, hoop-la!

Teddy Alright, we'll play hoop-la. God almighty, I'm getting drenched . . . (*Teddy uncovers the stall.*) Now, it says here, three rings for fifty p. Have you got fifty p?

† **Lucille** Fifty p? Non, je n'ai pas fifty p. Je n'ai pas d'argent sur moi.

Teddy You haven't got it? Well you'll have to owe me. You – owe – me. Here you are. (*He hands her three rings.*) Now, you've got to get them over these things. You know what to do?

Lucille (*throwing a ring wildly*) Voila!

Teddy Yes. I think the idea though is to get the ring somewhere in the vicinity of the table.

Lucille (*a similar wild throw*) Voila!

Teddy Yes, that killed the vicar, jolly good. One more!

   Lucille winds up for the big throw.

(*throwing himself flat*) No!

   The ring sails over his head.

‡ **Lucille** (*really enjoying herself*) Oh, j'adore cet orchestre. J'ai euvie de danser!

---

* Look! The hoop-la! I want to play hoop-la!

† Fifty p? No, I haven't got fifty p. I have no money on me.

‡ Oh, I love this band. I want to dance!

Teddy Don't for God's sake bowl for the pig, we'll have dead pork everywhere. Hey, hang about. Look what's here. (*He indicates the hoop-la table.*) A bottle of scotch. Le scotch – ici.

Lucille Whisky?

Teddy Yes, now watch this – I'll have a go for this one. (*taking up three more rings*) Watch this! Hup!

    He misses.

Damn!

* **Lucille** Ah, c'est nul. Recommencez!

Teddy (*trying again and missing*) Oh, bull nuts!

† **Lucille** Encore une fois! Encore une fois!

    Teddy throws again, misses, but Lucille guides the hoop safely over the scotch bottle.

‡ Bravo! Bien joué!

Teddy Oh, excellent stuff. By God, we make a fine team.

    He takes the bottle, removes the top and offers it to Lucille. She drinks long and thirstily.

(*alarmed*) Hang on, hang on! There are two of us, you know.

Lucille Agincourt!

Teddy Agincourt! Yes, indeed. (*He also drinks.*)

Lucille (*bounding on to the edge of the fountain*) Teddy! Teddy!

---

* Ah, no. Shame. Try again.

† Once more! Once more!

‡ Bravo! Well played!

Teddy Now what are you doing?

* **Lucille** Je vais nager dans le bassin.

Teddy What?

Lucille Pourquoi ça ne marche pas? La fontaine?

Teddy The fountain? It doesn't work. It hasn't worked for several years. We think it's clogged. Probably leaves, weeds and dead animals. Clogged.

† **Lucille** Clogged? (*kicking off her shoes*) Clogged. (*She starts to paddle in the fountain.*) Ah, c'est bon!

Teddy Aren't you wet enough? You're barking, woman.

Lucille Barking. Clogged. Allez, Teddy, venez faire trempette avec moi. (*She beckons.*)

Teddy I'm not getting in there.

Lucille Teddy! Teddy!

Teddy Oh, God. Alright. (*He takes off his shoes.*) I don't know what you're walking on. All sorts of nasty things. (*He steps into the fountain.*) Aaah! It's absolutely perishing. I'm not standing in this!

> *Teddy steps out again. During the next, he sits on the edge of the fountain, takes off his socks wrings them out, then puts them on again. Lucille also gets out, finds the whisky bottle, sits beside him and drinks.*

---

* **Lucille** I'm going to swim in your pond.

Teddy What?

Lucille Why doesn't it work? Your fountain?

† **Lucille** Clogged? (*kicking off her shoes*) Clogged. (*She starts to paddle in the fountain.*) Ah, this is good!

Teddy Aren't you wet enough? You're barking, woman.

Lucille Barking. Clogged. Come on, Teddy, paddle with me. (*She beckons.*)

Lucille (*ruffling his hair*) Teddy!

Teddy You know, just this short time I've known you . . . it's extraordinary. I'd forgotten what it's like to have a good laugh, you know. Everyone around me's so bloody serious. I've got a serious wife, I've a seriously serious daughter and I've just got shot of a mistress who was serious for Britain. Where's the fun gone, eh? You know what I'm saying? You see, I understood that the whole thing between men and women was somehow meant to be sort of joyous . . . and then you look around at all these miserable bastards. And you think why are you all bothering? If you're that miserable, why don't you just say piss off to each other and then just get on with having a spot of fun? You know what I'm saying? Take sex. It's a bloody brilliant invention, isn't it? It's all made to fit. This bit goes in there and everybody has a good time. But you read the bloody books and you'd think it was the university entrance exam. It's so depressing, it really is. And you feel yourself getting more and more crushed by it all. Guilty. And then someone like you passes through my life. I don't understand a bloody word you're saying, but I realise just for these few seconds how wonderful it all could have been. And could be again. You see?

* **Lucille** (*who has caught his mood*) Moi, qu'est-ce que j'ai fait de ma vie? J'avais de l'ambition. Je rêvais d'être une grande actrice, à la Comédie Française peut-être. Et je me retrouve à jouer une pépée d'Hollywood dans un petit film minable bourré de terroristes. Et même pas la pépée vedette. Ma plus grande scène, c'est celle où je

---

* Me? What's my life been like? I used to have ambitions. I used to want to be this great actress with the Comédie Française, perhaps. And I end up playing Hollywood crumpet in a tacky little film about terrorists. Not even the main crumpet. My biggest scene is where I get blown up. Only it isn't even me that's blown up. It's my stunt double. God, what a mess I've made

reçois une bombe en pleine figure. Et ce n'est même pas moi qui reçoit la bombe. C'est une doublure. Mon Dieu, quel gâchis ma vie. Deux maris, le premier m'a poussée à boire, le second à me droguer. Maintenant, regardez-moi. Dans quelques années, je ne ressemblerai à rien. Personne ne voudra plus de moi. Je ne vaudrai plus que dalle, ni au cinéma, ni même pour recevoir une bombe en pleine figure. Ah, si je vous avais recontré plus tôt, peut-être que les choses auraient été differéntes. Nous aurions peut-être trouvé le bonheur. Au moins, on serait morts en s'étouffant de rire. Mais maintenant, c'est trop tard. Je dois aller dans cette clinique, ça fait partie des conditions de ma liberté surveillée. Sinon j'irai en prison pour trafic de drogue. Et vous, vous allez rejoindre votre anglais collet-monté qui ne vous regarde même pas et refuse d'admetttre votre existence. Mon Dieu, quelle tristesse. Vous êtes gentil, Teddy. Idiot mais brave.

Teddy I don't think I've ever talked like this with anyone . . . thank you for listening to me, Lucille. And for saying that. I found it very moving.

† **Lucille** (*getting up and extending her hands*) Vous comprenez, n'est-ce-pas? Je sais que vous comprenez . . .

Teddy What?

---

of my life. Two husbands, one of whom drove me to drink, the other one introduced me to drugs. Now look at me. In a few years, I'll look like nothing. No one will want me. Not in any movies. I won't even be worth blowing up. Oh, if I'd met someone like you at the start, perhaps things might have been different. Perhaps we'd have found happiness. At least we'd have died laughing together. Now it's too late. I have to go to this clinic, because that's the terms of my probation. Otherwise I go to jail for drug trafficking. And you – you go back to your stuffy English wife who won't even look at you and refuses to acknowledge your existence. God, how sad. You're a sweet man, Teddy. A silly man but a good man.

† You understand, don't you? I know you understand . . .

Lucille Venez, Teddy. Dans ma tente.*

> *She takes his hands and pulls him to his feet. She starts to pull him towards the tent.*

Teddy Where are we going?

† **Lucille** Je suis Cléopâtre. Je vous emmène dans ma tente, Teddy . . .

Teddy Cleopatra? What's she got to do with anything?

‡ **Lucille** Vous êtes mon Marc-Antoine. Nous allons faire magnifiquement l'amour une dernière fois avant de mourir. Je suis votre Thisbe, vous êtes mon Pyrame. Vous êtes mon Tristan, je suis votre Isolde . . .

Teddy I don't know who any of these people are. Never mind . . .

Lucille (*drawing him into the tent*) Teddy . . .

Teddy Lucille . . .

Lucille Teddy . . .

> *They go into the tent. The band plays on.*
> *An initial cry from Lucille, then from Teddy.*
> *Suddenly, for the first time, the fountain makes a rusty gurgling sound and spurts into life.*
> *Izzie enters from the house. She stands and stares at the tent, listening to the sounds from within. After a moment, she dives for a box under the home-made cake table and finds a big vicious looking carving knife. She marches up to the tent. For a minute we*

---

* Come on, Teddy. Into my tent.

† I am Cleopatra. I am taking you into my tent, Teddy . . .

‡ You are my Mark Antony. We will make glorious love one last time before we die. I am your Thisbe, you are my Pyramus. You are my Tristan, I am your Isolde . . .

fear carnage, then she contents herself by sawing at the principle guy ropes. The tent collapses on the occupants. A cry of surprise from within. Pearl comes on with her camera. She stops as she sees Izzie.

Izzie (*realising her error*) Oh no, I done the wrong ones. Pearl – (*She moves towards Pearl.*)

Pearl (*in terror*) Get away! Get away! You get away from me!

Pearl rushes off. Izzie follows her.

Izzie Pearl, come back here. I didn't mean nothing . . . It was a miscopulation! (*Izzie goes off.*)

Teddy (*from under the collapsed tent*) My God, I think the earth moved for me!

* **Lucille** (*likewise*) Oh, mon Dieu! Quel amant! Qui dit que les anglais sont frigides!

Some movement under the canvas.

Teddy Can you get out?

† **Lucille** Non, je crois que je suis coincée. Il faudrait qu'on nous aide.

Teddy No, I don't think I can. (*struggling*) Har . . . har . . . no!

Warn comes on. He stops when he sees the fountain working. As Teddy and Lucille start to shout, he inspects the fallen tent.

We'll have to get some help. (*calling*) Help!

Lucille Help!

---

* Oh, my God! What a lover! Who says the English are frigid!

† No, I appear to be stuck. I think we need some help.

They continue to shout. Warn takes up one of the guy ropes and examines the cut end.

Warn Bloody women!

He strides off to the house, ignoring their cries.

Both (*continuing*) Help! . . . Help! . . .

Giles enters along one of the paths.
He hurries over.

Giles (*alarmed*) Hallo! Are you alright? Who's under here?

Teddy Who's that?

Giles I'm a doctor, can I help . . .?

Teddy Giles . . .

Giles Who's that?

Teddy It's me, Teddy.

Giles Teddy! Who's that with you?

* **Lucille** Hallo! Pouvez-vous nous aider? On est coincés là-dessous. Il faudrait qu'on nous délivre . . .

Giles Lucille?

Lucille Hallo.

Giles My God, I don't believe this. You're obscene, Teddy, you're utterly debauched. It's just one woman after another, isn't it, as far as you're concerned?

Teddy Look, spare us the bloody moral lecture, Giles, just get us out of here . . .

Fran enters from the house.

Fran What's happened?

---

* Hallo! Could you possibly help us? We appear to be a bit stuck under here and we need rescuing . . .

Giles The tent appears to have collapsed on them, I'm just –

Fran Who's under there? Lucille?

Giles Yes and Mr –

* **Fran** Lucille! Ça va?

Lucille Oui, ça va. On est juste un peu serrés . . .

Fran Attendez une seconde. Je vais vous sortir de là.

Lucille Merci!

Fran reaches under the tent and starts to pull Lucille out. The rain starts to ease off.

Fran (*to Giles*) Give me a hand here.

Giles Careful! They may have broken limbs . . .

Fran ignores this and together they pull Lucille clear.

† **Lucille** Ça va mieux! Vive la liberté! Où est Teddy?

Fran Comment vous sentez-vous? Vous allez bien?

Lucille Oh oui, je ne me suis jamais si bien sentie. Je n'ai pas fait l'amour comme ça depuis une éternité . . .

Fran On ferait mieux de rentrer à la maison, vous êtes trempée.

---

* **Fran** Lucille! Are you alright?
Lucille Yes, I'm fine. We're just a little squashed . . .
Fran Just a second, I'll pull you out.
Lucille Thank you!

† **Lucille** That's better! Free again! Where's Teddy?
Fran How are you feeling? Are you alright?
Lucille Yes, I've never felt better. I haven't made love like that in ages . . .
Fran We'd better get you back to the house, you're soaking wet.

* **Lucille** Non, je dois faire l'ouverture de la fête d'abord . . .

Fran Qu'ils aillent se faire voir avec leur fête. Je ne veux pas être responsable devant le bureau si vous attrapez une pneumonie . . .

Teddy I say, are you going to stop all that jabbering and rescue me, or what?

Giles (*reaching under the canvas*) It's alright, Teddy, I've got you. (*to Fran*) Would you mind?

Fran moves to assist him.

Alright, Teddy, now gently . . . Heave!

Teddy's head and shoulders appear.

Heave . . .

Teddy (*urgently*) Hold it! Hold it! Hold it a second!

Giles That hurting?

Teddy I think I may have a bit of a problem . . .

Giles Alright . . . (*to Fran*) Ease off, ease off . . . Where's the problem located, Teddy? Can you describe it?

Teddy It's just generally my – lower half.

Giles I see. (*sotto to Fran*) My God, it could be spinal . . . Teddy, lie there perfectly still, till there's more of us here to lift you . . .

† **Lucille** (*to Fran*) Il y a un problème?

Fran Le médecin pense qu'il a peut-être une blessure à la colonne vertébrale.

---

* **Lucille** No, I have to open their fete first . . .

Fran To hell with their fete, I'm not going to be answerable to the office if you catch pneumonia . . .

† **Lucille** (*to Fran*) What's the problem?

Fran The doctor thinks he may have a spinal injury.

Lucille Oh, mon Dieu! Ce n'est pas possible. (*kneeling by Teddy*) Teddy, vous êtes blessé?

Teddy Oh, hallo, old thing . . .

Giles Teddy, just lie still, please. It may be serious.

Teddy Right you are. In that case I wonder if I could have a final request?

Giles What?

Teddy Could you tell that bloody band to stop that din?

Giles Yes, of course. (*calling*) Could you stop playing, please? There's someone here been badly injured. Yes, stop! Thank you!

> *The band tails to a halt. From the house, Barry and the Maypole dancers appear.*

Barry (*alarmed*) What's happened? What on earth has happened?

† **Lucille** (*grasping Teddy's arm*) Le pauvre Teddy, il est blessé. Tout à l'heure il etait si heureux, et voila que maintenant . . .

Giles Please don't shake him around, he may be injured. Ne le secouez pas.

Barry Injured? How badly injured?

Giles We don't know. He was sheltering in the tent. It fell on him.

---

* Oh, my God! That's not possible. (*kneeling by Teddy*) Teddy, you're injured?

† **Lucille** (*grasping Teddy's arm*) Poor Teddy is injured. One minute he was so happy, the next . . .

Giles Please don't shake him around, he may be injured. Do not shake him.

Fran The doctor thinks he may have spinal injuries.

Barry Oh, my goodness!

* **Lucille** C'est de ma faute, c'est moi qui l'ai emmené sous la tente . . .

Barry Has someone summoned an ambulance? We need the paramedics.

Teddy No, I don't need a bloody ambulance. Don't call an ambulance whatever you do, for God's sake.

Barry He sounds delirious.

Teddy Do your bloody Maypole dance or something . . .

Giles Hardly the time for a Maypole dance, surely.

Barry Might be a good idea. Take his mind off the pain. If he has major spinal injuries . . .

Giles I never said that . . .

Barry Right. Come along, children. Time for the dance now . . .

Giles Oh, well. I'll see if I can find the cassette player. I put it somewhere.

As the dancers assemble round the Maypole, Lindy enters. Giles finds the cassette machine under a table and checks the tape.

Lindy What's happened?

Barry Ah! There you are. I'll tell you what's happened, Lindy. The tent which you put up and swore you had checked, has just fallen on Mr Platt.

Lindy Oh, no . . .

Barry As a result of which, he has multiple injuries to his lower body and may never walk again . . .

---

* It's my fault for taking him into the tent . . .

Giles Now, I never said . . .

Barry All of which is entirely down to you, Lindy. We could be in for a million pound lawsuit, do you realise that?

Lindy (*sitting on the grass*) Yes, alright, alright . . .

Barry All because you rush things, you don't concentrate, you're careless and never ever bother to check. Well, now it's home to roost, Lindy, as I said it would be. I'm going to get my mobile and phone an ambulance.

Barry goes off. Lindy sits in a miserable heap. Giles starts the cassette machine and the Maypole dance gets under way. The children start their routine, quite well at first, given the incongruous nature of the occasion.

The bushes rustle. Giles is aware of this but can't locate the sound.

Giles (*to Lindy*) I wouldn't worry too much. He'll be fine, I'm sure.

Lindy doesn't reply.

Grass is quite wet. Be careful . . .

Fran watches the dancers. At some stage Gavin enters from the house and also watches. Giles gives them gentle encouragement. Lucille decides to play The Death of Nelson with Teddy's prostrate body.

* **Lucille** Oh, Teddy. Je veux que vous sachiez, si vous n'en réchappez pas que vous êtes le meilleur amant que j'ai jamais eu . . . je me souviendrai toujours de vous, Teddy . . .

---

* Oh, Teddy. I want you to know, if you don't survive, you were the best lover I have ever had . . . I will remember you for ever, Teddy . . .

Teddy What are you on about now, you batty woman?

* **Lucille** Je ne vous oublierai jamais. Embrassez-moi encore une fois, Teddy. Oh, mon pauvre chéri. S'il vous arrivait quelques chose, je ne me le pardonnerais jamais . . . Je serai votre Brunhilde. Je me jetterai dans les flammes s'il vous arrivait quelque chose . . .

Teddy (*during her last*) I can't think of a more inappropriate way to die, I really can't . . .

As the dance continues, Lucille throws herself across Teddy's body and showers him with kisses.

Oh, I don't know though . . .

Suddenly the bushes part and there is Joanna, eyes blazing, a completely deranged figure. Wet and muddy from the rain, she looks more like the Swamp Creature. Everyone freezes.

Fran What the hell . . .?

Joanna (*focusing on Teddy*) Sebastian?

Teddy (*startled*) What?

Joanna Gotcha! (*rushing at him in a wild charge*) AAAAArrrrrhhhh!!!

Teddy Oh, my God!

Lindy screams. Lucille screams. The Maypole dancers panic and rush about getting hopelessly entangled. Giles takes a pace forward and kicks over the cassette machine which unaccountably goes into double speed.
Gavin watches, the disinterested bystander.
Joanna kicks Teddy through the canvas.

---

* I will never forget you. Kiss me one more time, Teddy. Oh, my poor darling. If anything's happened to you, I will never forgive myself . . . I will be your Brunhild. I will hurl myself into the flames if anything happens to you . . .

Joanna (*as she does so*) You bastard! Bastard! Bastard! Bastard!

Teddy Aaaah! What the hell are you doing! Jo! Jo!

Giles Joanna! For goodness sake!

Joanna (*kicking him again*) Bastard! Bastard!

* **Lucille** Ne donnez pas de coups de pieds à mon Teddy, petit salope!

> *Lucille attempts to pull Joanna away. Joanna wheels on her attacker and takes the fight to her. Barry returns during this and watches open-mouthed.*

Fran Hey! Hey! Hey!

Giles Come along, calm down, calm down.

> *Joanna throws herself at Lucille and the two start a hand to hand fight which Giles, Barry and Fran try to break up. Lindy attempts to disentangle the dancers. The band starts up again.*

† **Lucille** Ne me touchez pas, espèce de folle! Au secours! Elle est complètement folle!

> *Teddy, alarmed as anyone by this spectacle, gets up from under the tent. He is barefoot, in his underpants, without his trousers, but is otherwise completely unharmed.*

Barry Lindy, get the youngsters to safety. Get them away from here!

> *Lindy goes, shepherding the dancers.*

Teddy Now, break it up, that's quite enough of that. I'm not worth fighting over . . .

---

* Don't you kick my Teddy, you little bitch.

† Get your hands off me, you madwoman! Help me, someone! She's completely mad!

Joanna is finally overpowered.

Giles (*breathless*) It's alright! She's calmer now. I'll get her home. Don't worry. Leave her to me. I'll give her a sedative.

Barry You sure?

* **Fran** (*to Lucille*) Ça va?

Lucille Oui, ça va. Qu'est-ce-qui se passe? Ça fait partie de la fête?

Giles Come on, darling, home now. It's only me. It's Giles. Come on.

Joanna (*exhausted*) Giles? No, you're not Giles. You're Harold. You're Harold, I know you are . . .

Giles Well, maybe just temporarily, darling . . . Giles will be back in a minute, I promise.

Giles and Joanna go off. Everyone is suddenly aware of Teddy's state of undress.

Lucille (*delighted*) Oh, Teddy!

Barry Well, I'm delighted to see that there was no damage done, Teddy. No bones broken . . . (*He too stares, the last to notice Teddy.*)

Teddy No. Extraordinary freak accident. You'll hardly believe this. Quite remarkable. We were standing in the tent sheltering from the rain. And the thing suddenly collapsed on us. And as it did so, the central pole, you follow me, the central pole as it fell, caught in the waist band of my trousers and ripped them off like that. Extraordinary.

A silence.

---

* **Fran** (*to Lucille*) Are you alright?

Lucille Yes, I'm alright. What was that about? Was it part of the fete?

Do excuse me. I'm just going to rout out another pair. Excuse me. (*to Lucille*) You coming up to the house to dry off? Dry off?

Lucille Dry off? Oui.

Teddy Come on then. My little bonbon . . .

Teddy and Lucille go off. Lindy returns.

Lindy They're all safely in the mini-van.

Fran There is an additional feature to all this. Which I didn't like to mention.

Barry What's that?

Fran Someone's deliberately cut these guy ropes. (*holding up a severed rope*) Look at that.

Barry My goodness. Foul play, you think?

Fran Worth considering, eh?

Fran goes. Barry inspects the ropes.

Barry (*to Lindy*) Well. There's a turn up for the book, eh? Yes. Well. Puts us in the clear, anyway, doesn't it? That's a relief. Oh, Mr Ryng-Mayne, I didn't see you there. You staying for a bit of the fun?

Gavin Sadly, I have to be under way pretty soon.

Barry Ah. Busy man. If you have a minute to spare, before you go, I wonder if you'd mind very much judging the junior fancy dress?

Gavin Ah, well . . .

Barry It won't take a moment of your time. I was going to ask Lucille – but she's – rather indisposed at present. It would be a great thrill for them, if you would . . . I'll just assemble them – I'll be back in a minute . . .

Barry goes off before Gavin can protest.

Gavin (*to himself*) Oh, God.

Lindy Excuse me . . .

Gavin Hallo, there.

Lindy That is your car, isn't it? The yellow one?

Gavin Yes. Sorry, is it blocking someone, I'll . . .?

Lindy I couldn't help overhearing you saying you'll be leaving soon.

Gavin Yes, I'm afraid I've –

Lindy Would that be back to London, would it?

Gavin That's right.

Lindy Would you . . . I know this sounds very cheeky of me but – would you be able to give me a lift?

Gavin Where to?

Lindy To London.

Gavin Oh, I see. (*searching for an excuse*) Well . . .

Lindy I wouldn't ask normally, but it is a matter of great urgency . . .

Gavin I see. It's important you go tonight, is it?

Lindy Very important. If I don't go tonight, I may not go at all, you see.

Gavin (*rather mystified*) I see. Well, I hope you don't have a lot of luggage – ?

Lindy Oh, I've got no luggage at all. Not so's you'd mention.

Gavin Right. Well, I'll be setting off in about an hour, so . . .

Lindy (*as she goes*) I'll be waiting. I'll be by the car.

Gavin Right.

Lindy goes off.

(*to himself*) God.

Barry returns.

Barry Here we all are. Parade across, children. Let Mr
Ryng-Mayne get a good look at you.

*An assortment of small fancy dress figures parade on
and off again. Gavin looks appalled.*

There! Hard to choose, eh? Hard to choose?

Gavin Almost impossible. What a magnificent turnout.
Well done, chaps.

Barry Come and take a closer look. (*following them off*)
By the way, don't choose the letter-box, he won last year.

Gavin (*as he goes off*) Oh, my God . . .

As they go, the lights fade to:
  Blackout.

SCENE TWO

Saturday, August 14th, 5.00 p.m.
  *The same, though it has been tidied up a bit. The
collapsed tent is gone. The band has stopped playing.*
  *Giles and Jake are packing away the Maypole, which
is now lying on its side. Giles is still in his Morris outfit.
Jake's briefcase is nearby.*

Giles I didn't think they were going to score at all . . .

Jake Nor did I . . .

Giles The last ten minutes, though . . .

Jake Amazing . . .

Giles Did you see that final cross, the one that eventually went in? I mean he was practically behind the net. I thought he's overshot, he'll never bring it back from there . . . never . . .

Jake Amazing . . .

Giles I don't know, then he managed to just curl it, didn't he? Beautiful cross. I mean, the keeper was way out of position, wasn't he? No way . . . Wish I'd been there.

Jake Amazing . . .

Giles We needed it.

Silence.

Jake I suppose we ought to talk about Mum, really.

Giles Yes, yes. I suppose we should.

Jake I mean, what's going to happen, Dad?

Giles Well, I think we just – have to see her back to health. I think it might take some time but we can do it. We can do it. She needs patience, she needs understanding, she needs – love. That's all. And I suppose if that means answering to the name of Harold for a month or two, that's what it'll have to be. I wish to God she'd chosen some other name.

Jake I'm not too keen on Gordon, actually.

Giles I keep saying we, Jake. But I want you to understand this is not primarily your problem.

Jake She's my mother, for God's sake . . .

Giles Yes. But what's happened to Jo – it's none of your doing . . .

Jake It's nobody's doing . . .

Giles It's down to me, Jake. It's all down to me.

Jake Look, Mum has an illness, that's all . . . Nobody's to blame. I mean, she needs professional help, surely?

Giles And she'll get professional help, don't worry. I'm making enquiries first thing tomorrow. Well, on Monday. She'll get the best, Jake. Don't worry.

Jake I just don't want you worrying yourself to death. I mean, by taking unnecessary blame. You're a good person. Bloody hell, I'm sure you drove her nuts on occasions, but you're a good person.

Giles (*quite touched*) Thank you. No, what I'm really trying to say, Jake, is that you mustn't get yourself too embroiled in all this. It is my problem. Really it is. And I promise I won't let it all get on top of me more than's absolutely vital. But you've got a life of your own to lead. You've got university in a few weeks, you've got to think about a career – I don't know – you've got Sally perhaps – I don't know . . .

Jake (*dryly*) Ha, ha, ha . . .

Giles No, don't give up on that. I think she likes you, you know . . .

Jake Yes. So people keep telling me. Only person who doesn't tell me is her.

Giles Well . . . Ever thus, eh?

Jake I'm going to give it one more go in a minute . . .

Giles Ah. Worked out a strategy?

Jake You bet. I'm going to get down as far as her goal line and then send her a deep swirling cross, right in front of her net. Catch her out of position.

Giles That should do it.

Jake Won't stand a chance. Right. Well. See you later, then . . . (*He picks up his briefcase.*)

Barry comes on briefly.

Barry Nobody's seen my wife, have they? Anyone here seen Lindy?

Giles Not for some little while.

Jake No.

Barry Unbelievable. I've had to load that whole van on my own. Lindy's completely vanished. If you do happen to see her, would you tell her I have now driven home where I will be unloading the van single-handed. I will then be back here in forty-five minutes to pick up the second load. And that I would be eternally grateful on that occasion for a modicum of her help. And she might be interested to know that I think my back is playing up again as well. If you could tell her all of that. Thank you.

Barry goes off.

Giles I wonder if I should nip down to the village and get Joanna some herbal bath crystals. I might persuade her to have a bath when she wakes up. Help to ease some of her tension.

Jake Why don't you just go and get pissed, Dad? Go on, treat yourself. (*Jake goes off towards the house.*)

Giles Now, what's that ever solved, Jake? What's that ever solved, eh?

Giles picks up the tape recorder. He removes the cassette tape, is about to put it away, then he reads the label on the other side. He replaces the cassette and plays it. Some suitable Morris dance music. Giles smiles rather regretfully and is about to switch it off

when Pearl arrives. She has changed out of her
fortune-teller's gear. Giles switches off the music.

Pearl Not goin' to get a dance then, aren't we?

Giles (*smiling*) Alas, no. I'm afraid the rest of my troop
are in Peterborough, would you believe? They finally
phoned me at four-fifteen. A cross-booking. Nobody let
me know.

Pearl Shame.

Giles Yes. It was.

Pearl Like a dance, do you?

Giles It's – rewarding, yes. Some people think it's rather
quaint. Comical, even. But they're very powerful these
dances. Some of them. Go back a long way. Fourteenth
century. Edward III.

Pearl Whey-hey!

Giles And before that probably from Spain . . .

Pearl Olé . . . Do us a bit, then. Go on.

Giles I can't. There's only me.

Pearl Come on. No one's watching. I'd like to see a bit.
Honest.

Giles (*a little uncertain as to whether she's sending him
up*) Well . . . It'll look a bit silly but . . . Just a little
section. (*He switches on the tape. He begins to dance, a
little self-consciously at first. It does, as he says, look a
bit silly but Pearl is entranced.*) You have to imagine
there's about sixteen of us doing this, not just me.

> *After a time, Pearl joins in. Although her dancing has
> no relation to any known Morris step, the result is not
> displeasing. Fran comes from the house, crosses and
> goes off staring at them curiously. As they dance,*

215

Gavin appears from the direction of the house. He watches, amused. The dance on the tape finishes.

Pearl Hey! That were great.

Giles Well, I'm rather glad my colleagues weren't here. I might have been drummed out of the United Kingdom Morris Federation . . .

Pearl Don't allow women, then?

Giles Oh yes, indeed. There's a lot of female Morris dancers. We're totally liberated these days . . .

Gavin Like the MCC.

Giles Oh, hallo.

Gavin (*clapping them*) Well done. Jolly good.

Pearl Well, I must get on. Thanks for the dance. Going for a drink later. Want to join us?

Giles Us?

Pearl Just a few of us. Me, my mum. And my dad.

Giles Your dad? I didn't know you'd – ?

Pearl Warn. He's my dad.

Giles Is he? Good heavens, I – I think a lot of people thought he was – well –

Pearl Nar. That wouldn't be right, would it? Not with me own dad.

Giles No, certainly not.

Pearl Want to come?

Giles (*torn*) Ah, well . . . probably not. My wife's a bit under the . . . Normally I'd love to –

Pearl We'll be in the Wheatsheaf if you do. Beer's piss down The Plough . . .

Giles Right. Thank you very much. I'll see what I can arrange.

Pearl Cheers, then.

Giles Bye.

Gavin Good-bye.

Pearl goes off.

Sounds a tempting invitation. I think you're in there with a chance.

Giles (*laughing inordinately*) Oh, good heavens. Hardly! Hardly! You're off, are you?

Gavin Afraid so. It's been a marvellous afternoon. Thoroughly enjoyed myself.

Giles The weather was a little disappointing, I'm afraid. I don't think we did financially as well as we'd hoped. Well, have a safe journey. Shouldn't take you long in that thing of yours . . .

Gavin About twenty five minutes, I should think. Ciao.

Giles 'Bye.

Giles goes off. Gavin is about to go when Lindy steps out from the bushes into his path. She has a small case.

Lindy Hallo.

Gavin (*rather put out*) Ah –

Lindy Here I am. All ready.

Gavin Yes. Right. Is that – all your luggage? Because I have limited boot space . . .

Lindy No, this all I'm taking.

Gavin Just a short visit, is it?

Lindy No.

Gavin Ah.

Lindy But I'm taking as little as possible.

Gavin (*completely mystified*) I see.

Lindy Then I can't be accused of taking anything, you see.

Gavin I should warn you, when I travel I like to put my foot down.

Lindy I won't be any trouble, I promise.

Gavin No, no, no. I like to travel at speed. You're comfortable with high speeds, are you?

Lindy The faster the better.

Gavin And there'll be a bit of a din. You don't mind loud noise?

Lindy Oh, no. I'm used to that. Our old Transit makes a dreadful racket, I think it's the gearbox . . .

Gavin No, what I meant was, I'll be playing rather loud music. OK?

Lindy Classical?

Gavin No. Late 'sixties – 'seventies rock. Is that OK?

Lindy Oh, yes. The Monkees?

Gavin (*wincing*) Along those lines, yes . . . Well, off we go. After you and fasten your seat belt.

He ushers Lindy ahead of him.

(*as they go*) God!

As they leave, Fran returns rattling her car keys rather impatiently. From the direction of the house, Teddy's voice is heard.

Teddy (*off*) It's alright! She's coming, she's coming.

Lucille (*off*) I'm coming!

Teddy (*off*) I was just showing her our gazebo.

Lucille (*off*) Gazebo!

Teddy and Lucille enter.

Teddy Do you know, the poor girl had no idea what a gazebo was. Can you imagine? She's led a completely sheltered life . . .

* **Fran** I said we'd be there by six, we're going to be very late. (*to Lucille*) On va être en retard.

Lucille Oh, ne dites pas de sotises. Comment peut-être en retard pour faire un régime sec, Teddy? Au'voir. On se reverra bientôt.

Teddy Absolutely. And I'll write to you.

Lucille Vous êtes sans aucun doute l'homme le plus bête que j'aie jamais rencontré.

Teddy Thank you. Thank you.

Lucille Vraiment l'anglais le plus bête. Mais je vous aime. Vous êtes normalement une nation si solennelle, si pompeuse. Tellement sérieuse sur tout.

---

* **Fran** I said we'd be there by six, we're going to be very late. (*to Lucille*) We're going to be late.

Lucille Oh, nonsense. How can I be late to go on the wagon? Teddy. Au 'voir. We shall meet again, soon.

Teddy Absolutely. And I'll write to you.

Lucille You are without doubt the silliest man I have ever met.

Teddy Thank you. Thank you.

Lucille Certainly the silliest Englishman. But I love you. You are usually such a solemn, pompous nation. So serious about everything.

Teddy Yes, well, it could have been nicer, but that's the English climate for you, I'm afraid . . .

* **Lucille** Mais vous avez prouvé qu'ils avaient tort. Je me souviendrai de vous pendant longtemps. Je reviendrai, Teddy, aussitôt que je serai guérie, et on fera l'amour ensemble dans toutes vos drôles les petites cabanes de jardin. Oui?

Teddy You betcha. (*to Fran*) What's she saying?

Fran I don't think you should know. Not at the moment, we'd never get away from here. (*to Lucille*) Allez, venez s'il vous plaît.

Lucille Ne venez pas plus loin avec moi, Teddy. Restez-là, c'est ça. Laissez-moi vous embrasser – (*She kisses him.*) – et puis partir. Nous serons comme Philémon et Baucis, Teddy. Nous nous aimerons dans ce jardin et puis, quand nous serons morts, nous serons transformés par les dieux. Vous deviendrez un chêne, et moi je deviendrai un tilleul, et nos branches s'entrelaceront pour toujours. Alors, mon amour, au revoir.

Teddy Good-bye. I don't know what the hell you're talking about but by God you're beautiful when you say it . . .

---

* **Lucille** But you have proved them wrong. I shall remember you for a long time. I'll be back, Teddy, as soon as I'm cured and we shall make love together in all your funny little garden sheds. Yes?

Teddy You betcha. (*to Fran*) What's she saying?

Fran I don't think you should know. Not at the moment, we'd never get away from here. (*to Lucille*) Come on, please.

Lucille Don't come any further with me, Teddy. Stand just there, that's it. Let me kiss you – (*She kisses him.*) – and then walk away. We will be like Philemon and Baucis, Teddy. We will love each other in this garden and then, when we die, we will be transformed by the gods. You will become an oak tree and I will become a linden and our branches will intertwine forever. Good, my love, good bye.

Lucille Au revoir.

Fran Cheers.

> *Lucille goes off with Fran.*
> *Teddy watches them go rather sadly.*

Teddy Right then. Right.

> *He stands, undecided what to do. Barry appears*
> *briefly.*

Barry Any sign of her yet?

Teddy Who?

Barry Day of the vanishing wives, isn't it? Unbelievable. This is unbelievable. We're going to have to have serious words about this . . .

> *Barry goes. Teddy sits on the edge of the fountain.*
> *Giles comes across. He has changed into his normal*
> *clothes.*

Giles Oh. Don't mind if I cut across, do you?

Teddy Help yourself.

Giles I'm off to the pub. The Wheatsheaf. Beer's piss down The Plough. I'd invite you along, Teddy, but I'm sorry I think it will be another day or two before I can actually sit and drink with you.

Teddy That's alright. I don't fancy drinking with you either, just at present.

Giles Fair enough. Oh, Trish just passed me in her car. She told me, if I saw you, to say cheerio. That you'd know what she meant.

Teddy Oh, yes. I know what she meant.

Giles Well, cheerio, then.

Teddy Cheerie-bye.

> *He sits and whistles mournfully.*
> *Nearby, the sound of Spoof barking.*

Ah, there you are, boy. Somebody let you out, did they?
Good boy! Come on, here we are! Come on! Come to
daddy, come on! That's it! Come-boy, come-boy, come-
boy . . . Ah.

> *Spoof's barking recedes as he runs off into the*
> *distance. Teddy droops a little lower.*
> *Silence.*
> *Quite suddenly, there is a gurgling sound and the*
> *fountain behind him splutters and shuts off.*

(*looking at it, resignedly*) Ah, well. That's life, I suppose.

> *As he continues to sit there, contemplating his lot, the*
> *lights fade to:*
> *Blackout.*